STORIES WORTH READING

Skills Worth Learning

BOOK 2

BETSY CASSRIEL, SANTA BARBARA CITY COLLEGE

GAIL REYNOLDS, SANTA BARBARA CITY COLLEGE

THOMSON

HEINLE

United Kingdom I United States I Australia I Canada I Mexico I Singapore I Spain

THOMSON

HEINLE

Stories Worth Reading: Skills Worth Learning 2

Betsy Cassriel and Gail Reynolds

Publisher: *James W. Brown*
Senior Acquisitions Editor: *Sherrise Roehr*
Director of Product Development: *Anita Raducanu*
Associate Development Editor: *Tom Jefferies*
Editorial Assistant: *Katherine Reilly*
Director of Marketing: *Amy Mabley*
Marketing Manager: *Laura Needham*
Production Editor: *Chrystie Hopkins*
Technology Manager: *Andrew Christensen*

Senior Print Buyer: *Mary Beth Hennebury*
Compositor: *Dutton & Sherman Design*
Photo Researcher: *Dutton & Sherman Design*
Illustrator: *Meredith A. Morgan*
Cover/Text Designer: *Dutton & Sherman Design*
Printer: *Malloy*

Cover Image: *© PINTO/Masterfile*

Printed in the United States of America
1 2 3 4 5 6 7 8 9 10 ? 09 08 07 06 05

For more information contact Thomson Heinle, 25 Thomson Place, Boston, Massachusetts 02210 USA, or you can visit our Internet site at http://elt.thomson.com

ISBN: 1-4130-0856-9

Library of Congress Control Number
2004116291

CONTENTS

SCOPE AND SEQUENCE

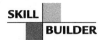

Stories Worth Reading: Skills Worth Learning 2 is a student-centered English language learning textbook containing interesting readings and communicative activities. *Stories Worth Reading: Skills Worth Learning 2* creates an interactive learning environment in which students have opportunities to build not only reading skills but also all-around communicative competence. Themes of courage, perseverance, and empowerment are woven throughout each of the eight units. The text is intended for students at the 1,000-word level.

STORIES WORTH READING . . .

Stories Worth Reading: Skills Worth Learning 2 contains fresh reading passages relevant to students' lives. The readings range from engaging true stories, to articles, to poems, and beyond. The text also includes maps and charts to broaden students' reading experiences.

Part One
Part One features a high-interest true story written with controlled vocabulary and sentence structure appropriate to this level. The vocabulary and sentence structure increases in complexity as the book progresses.

Part Two and Part Three
Part Two and Part Three include readings thematically related to Part One. Readings in Part Two are factual and are generally the most challenging of the three. This type of reading is aimed at teaching students to read for gist. A variety of more informal or personal readings such as emails, poems, essays and fiction are included in Part Three. These readings are extensions of the unit topics and help students become familiar with a wide range of reading genres.

. . . SKILLS WORTH LEARNING!

Not only does the *Stories Worth Reading: Skills Worth Learning 2* support student learning of appropriate reading skills, it also builds word study and communication skills.

Reading Skills
Ample practice with good reading skills such as finding main ideas and details, sequencing events, inferring, predicting, skimming and scanning follows each reading. A wide variety of exercises teach students how to approach different tasks. Pre-reading activities activate students' background knowledge, introduce vocabulary and relate the unit topic personally to the student.

Word Study Skills
Each unit teaches key vocabulary necessary to understanding each reading and on words that are useful for students at this level. Students review words in the original context, and practice words in new contexts.

Skill Builder

Icons throughout the text focus on specific reading and word study skills relevant to students at this level. The Skill Builder feature empowers students with better understanding of and practice with good reading skills. Examples of the reading Skill Builders are: skimming, summarizing, drawing conclusions, and distinguishing fact and opinion. In addition, the Skill Builder feature gives students an understanding of and practice with word-study skills. Examples of the word-study Skill Builders are: parts of speech, synonyms and antonyms, prefixes, suffixes dictionary skills, and word webs.

Communication Skills

Opportunities for developing all-around communicative competence and responding to readings in personally meaningful ways are found in the Communicating Your Ideas section. Students interact with one another and with the text through various speaking and writing activities. These engaging activities may involve small group discussion, letter writing, playing games, role-playing or sharing personal stories. While these activities offer practice with vocabulary and grammar, they are also intended to foster an environment of cooperation and community in the classroom.

Synthesis of Skills

The One Step Beyond section at the end of each unit offers exciting suggestions of multi-skill expansion activities to extend learning outside the classroom. There are recommendations for topic-related movies, guest speakers, songs, field trips and community organizations as well as assignments for journals, interviews, projects, Internet and library research and more.

A SCIENTIFICALLY BASED RESEARCH APPROACH

Skills Worth Reading: Skills Worth Learning 2 is based on current, scientifically based research findings of the most effective means to teach reading skills to adult and young adult learners of English.

Learner-Centered Content

Van Duzer (1999) emphasizes that research on adult ESL students shows that "learners should read texts that meet their needs and are interesting." In *Stories Worth Reading* readings are carefully selected so that they are both high-interest and relevant to the needs of adults.

Development of Reading Skills and Strategies

Grabe (1995) and Oxford (1990) assert that explicit instruction in reading skills and strategies helps adults improve their reading comprehension. *Stories Worth Reading* integrates explicit reading instruction and highlights key skills using the Skill Builder feature.

Development of New Language

Eskey (1997) emphasizes the importance of adult learners understanding the vocabulary and grammar they encounter as they read. Anderson (1999) suggests that basic vocabulary should be explicitly taught in conjunction with teaching students other strategies for less frequently encountered items. As such, each unit of *Stories Worth Reading* provides two word study Skill Builders which demonstrate and offer practice of vocabulary and grammar skills.

Using Background Knowledge

Because research shows that background knowledge facilitates comprehension (Eskey 1997) each unit of *Stories Worth Reading* opens with a photo montage, pictures, discussions, and quizzes and more related to the unit theme.

Multiple Intelligences and Diverse Learning Styles

As illustrated by Gardner et al (1996) intelligence is composed of at least seven components. *Stories Worth Reading* was developed to be compatible with learners' multiple intelligences by incorporating graphic organizers (spatial), hands-on projects (kinesthetic), and discussion questions (inter/intrapersonal)

Anderson, N. (1999). *Exploring second language reading: Issues and Strategies*. Boston: Thomson Heinle.

Eskey, D. (1997) Models of reading and the ESOL student. Focus on Basics 1 (B), 9-11.

Gardenr, H., Kornhaber, M., & Wake, W. (1996). *Intelligence: Multiple perspectives*. Fort Worth, TX: Harcourt Brace.

Grabe, W. (1995). Dilemmas for the development of second language reading abilities. *Prospect*, 10 (2), 38-51.

Oxford, R.L. (1990). *Language learning strategies: What every reader should know*. Boston: Thomson Heinle.

VanDuzer, C. (1999). Reading and the Adult Language Learner. ERIC Digest. Washington D.C.: National Center for ESL Literacy Education.

Getting Ready

Each unit starts with a Getting Ready activity that activates students' background knowledge and stimulates their interest in the topic. Small groups or partners work together in class on these interactive activities.

Pre-reading

Pre-reading activities before each reading prepare students to read. They are communicative and designed to be completed in class before a reading is assigned. Small groups or pairs share their findings with the class.

Reading and Word Study Skills

The readings and their accompanying comprehension and vocabulary exercises can be assigned as homework so that class time is maximized for interaction. In the next class students can correct exercises, clarify new vocabulary words and their pronunciation and retell the story. Alternatively, students can do this section in class and discuss the answers to the questions in groups. All the readings are available on the Audio Tape and CD that accompany this text.

Skill Builders

Teacher and students work together in class to build understanding and practice the reading and word skills presented in Skill Builders.

Communicating Your Ideas

Communicating Your Ideas activities help students relate story themes to themselves and to others, exploring their ideas about the topic. These speaking activities are to be used in class with small groups and pairs. **Write About It** writing assignments, which students can do as homework and then share with classmates. The reading passages and follow-up activities act as prewriting exercises for the writing activities.

For the **Talk About It** discussion questions students should be in groups of 3 or 4, sitting in a circle facing one another. Cooperative learning groups, in which students are assigned roles, work well. For a group of four students the roles might be discussion leader, spokesperson, recorder and timekeeper. Groups report back to the class with the help of graphic organizers such as newsprint, transparencies, charts, drawings, etc. We have great success keeping students in the same groups or "teams" for several weeks and even an entire semester. Groups may be formed randomly, by student choice or teacher choice.

One Step Beyond activities can be plugged in at any point in each unit. In fact, many of these activities are assignments that may take students a week or more to complete. Some take advance planning on the teacher's part. We suggest that as a teacher becomes familiar with the text at the beginning of the semester, she reads all of the One Step Beyond pages immediately. Then she can take advantage of these opportunities by planning ahead of time. These activities can be completed by the entire class, small groups, partners or individuals. We've had wonderful success in our classes giving students a number of different choices and then having them share presentations with the class.

ACKNOWLEDGMENTS

The publisher would like to thank the following individuals who offered helpful feedback and suggestions on the text:

Mona Brantley
Des Moines Area Community College, Des Moines, IA

Janeece Docal
Bell Multicultural Senior High School, Washington, DC

Diane Frangie
Fordson High School, Dearborn, MI

Virginia Guleff
Miramar College, San Diego, CA

Arnulfo Lopez
Delano High School, Delano, CA

Dr. Karen Morante
LaSalle University/BUSCA, Philadelphia, PA

We thank Sherrise Roehr for understanding and believing in our project and Tom Jefferies for embracing our vision, adding his own wonderful ideas and focusing an otherwise untamed work.

Thanks go to Victoria and Randy Rightmire, my dad, Marit ter-Mate Martinsen, Joe Thompson and Suzy Melin and Leona friends and family who generously shared their life stories with us and enthusiastically supported the project.

This book is lovingly dedicated to Wayne, Christopher and baby Brian.

ENGLISH EVERYWHERE

GETTING READY

1. Look at the people in the pictures. They are all learning English as a
   Second Language. What are they doing in each picture? Why do you think
   these people want to learn English?

2. Why do you want to learn English? Write three sentences. Share your
   sentences with your classmates.

   Example: *I want to learn English because I want to have my own business.*

   1. _____

   2. _____

   3. _____

A PASSION FOR ENGLISH

PRE-READING

1. The paragraphs below are from the story about Marit. Read the paragraphs. Put them into the correct order.

<table>
<tr>
<td>
Paragraph_____
In London, Marit made friends from other countries. They spoke English together. Soon she loved English.
</td>
<td>
Paragraph_____
When Marit was 17 years old, she went to London, England.
</td>
</tr>
<tr>
<td>
Paragraph_____
In high school, Marit learned English. She didn't like her English classes.
</td>
<td>
Paragraph_____
When she was 19 years old, she went to study English at a college in the United States.
</td>
</tr>
<tr>
<td>
Paragraph_____
Four years later, the college gave her a jos as an English teacher.
</td>
<td>
Paragraph___1___
Marit grew up in the Netherlands. Marit's mother is German, and her father is Dutch.
</td>
</tr>
</table>

2. Now read the story. Check if you put the paragraphs in the correct order.

A PASSION FOR ENGLISH

Marit grew up in the Netherlands. She is bilingual because her mother is German and her father is Dutch. Marit's neighbors were from all over the world. She liked talking to them. In high school, Marit studied English, but it was difficult for her. She didn't like her English classes. They didn't practice conversation. Marit wanted to learn to speak English so she could learn about people from different cultures.

Marit decided to study in an English-speaking country. She went to school in London when she was seventeen years old. School was expensive. She looked for a job, but her English was not good. She found a job at a fast food restaurant. Marit made many mistakes at her job because of her English. She didn't understand the customers. One day, her supervisor said, "Please mop the floor." Marit swept the floor! She needed to practice speaking English more.

Every day, Marit was tired from speaking and listening to English. Sometimes she spent a lot of time with her Dutch friends. Finally, she made a promise to herself. She said, "I will only see my Dutch friends once a week. I will speak more English." Marit was self-disciplined. She made new friends from other countries. They spoke English together. Marit often went shopping. She spoke English to people in stores. Soon she became comfortable speaking English. English sounded beautiful to her.

When she was nineteen years old, Marit made a plan. She decided to study at a college in the United States. At first, the classes were very hard for her. She was not good at reading and writing in English. But Marit had strategies to learn more English. She learned to use the dictionary. Every day, she went to the Writing Center. She asked the tutors many questions. Marit talked about books with her new friends. She also watched soap operas on television every day.

Marit graduated four years later. She was very proud. She was fluent in English! The college gave her a job as an English teacher, and then she married her American boyfriend a year later. Her hard work and passion gave her a new future. Today, Marit tells her English students, "Hard work and passion pay off!"

READING AND WORD STUDY SKILLS

A. Understanding the Main Ideas

Read the statements below. Circle T for true or F for false.

1. Marit likes to talk with people from other cultures.   T   F

2. English was difficult for Marit.   T   F

3. Marit did not study in English-speaking countries.   T   F

4. Marit had special ways for learning English.   T   F

5. Marit became fluent in English.   T   F

B. Finding Details

What strategies did Marit use to learn English?

Example: *Marit made new friends.*

1. _____

2. _____

3. _____

4. _____

5. _____

C. Learning New Words

Write the correct word next to the definition.

~~fluent~~	customers	bilingual	hard
proud	studied	decided	comfortable
self-disciplined	pay off		

1. can speak or write a language very well _____*fluent*_____

2. people who buy from a business _____

3. reached a conclusion _____

4. pleased, satisfied _____

5. difficult _____

6. feeling something is all right _____

7. learned _____

8. knowing two languages _____

9. to get a good result _____

10. the ability to work hard without needing someone else to make it happen _____

D. Using New Words

Complete each sentence with the correct word from exercise C.

1. I am _____ speaking in front of lots of people.

2. My friend is _____ in French, German and English.

3. Yi Ting did not like her job. She _____ to look for a new job.

4. My son got very good grades this year. I am _____ of him.

5. There was a big sale at the store. Many _____ were waiting in line.

6. My mother has two jobs. She works very _____.

7. My sister _____ psychology at school.

8. Doing homework and visiting tutors _____. You can learn a lot and get really good grades.

9. Marit was _____ as a child. She spoke two languages.

10. Bruno is _____. He works out at the gym every morning at five o'clock.

E. Your Dictionary

Marit used a dictionary when she learned English. A dictionary can help you with definitions of words, how to use them, how to spell them and how to pronounce them. Using a dictionary is important when learning a language.

1. Look at the Newbury House Dictionary entry below for *passion* and
   answer the questions.

> **pas·sion** /ˈpæʃən/ *n.* [C;U] **1** a strong, over-
> powering feeling, such as love, anger, or ha-
> tred: *He felt such a passion that he forgot
> where he was.*‖*She spoke with passion about
> the love of freedom.* **2** strong devotion to some
> activity: *She has a passion for painting.*
> **3 Passion:** (in Christianity) the suffering and
> death of Jesus: *Christians honor the Passion
> at Easter.*
>
> **passion 1** a strong emotion, intensity |
> fervor, ardor **2** zeal, a great love of s.t. *Ants.*
> indifference, apathy.

   a. What part of speech is *passion*?   noun   verb   adjective

   b. Circle the first definition of *passion*.

   c. Draw a line to the second definition of *passion*.

   d. Underline the third definition of *passion*.

   e. Write definition 1, 2 or 3 next to each sentence.

   _____ I have a passion for speaking English.

   _____ He has a strong passion for his wife.

   _____ In my Mexican town, we are celebrating the
   Passion this week.

2. Look at the dictionary entry for *proud* and answer the questions

> **proud** /praʊd/ *adj.* **1** pleased, satisfied with an
> accomplishment: *She was proud that she had
> won the race.* **2** dignified, showing self-
> esteem: *That family is too proud to accept
> money from charity, even though they are very
> poor.* **3** arrogant, rude: *He is too proud to be a
> good friend to anyone.* See: pride.
>
> **proud 1** delighted, gratified. *Ant.*
> embarrassed. **2** principled **3** conceited,
> egotistical | defiant. *Ants.* humble, modest.

   a. What part of speech is *proud*?   noun   verb   adjective

   b. Write definition 1, 2 or 3 next to each sentence.

_____ Marit was proud when she graduated.

_____ That footballer is too proud. He thinks he is better than his teammates.

_____ The old man is too proud to accept help.

3. Use your dictionary to check one or two other words you don't know in *A Passion for English*. Share the words and their meanings with your class.

COMMUNICATING YOUR IDEAS

A. Write About It

Marit used many different strategies to learn English. What strategies can *you* use to learn English? Write four strategies below. Discuss your strategies with your classmates.

Example: *I can ask the teacher questions after class.*

1. _____

2. _____

3. _____

4. _____

B. Interviewing

Walk around your classroom and ask your classmates about their passions. Write their names in the correct box.

Example: *"Do you have a passion for sports?" "Yes, I do./No, I don't."*

music	travel	sports	movies	English	_____

YOU SAY TOMATO, I SAY TOMATO!

PRE-READING

1. Look at the map on page 9. Name five countries where people speak English as an official language. Is your teacher from one of these countries?

2. Is the English language different from country to country? If yes, can you give examples?

READING AND WORD STUDY SKILLS

A. Understanding the Main Ideas

Skimming means to read quickly. You don't need to know every word. You skim to get the main idea about an article. Skimming helps you become a more fluent reader.

Skim the article. Circle the correct answer.

1. English is spoken

    a. in a lot of places.
    b. in a small number of places.

2. British English is

    a. the same as American English.
    b. different from American English.

3. More people in the world speak

    a. Mandarin Chinese.
    b. English.

YOU SAY TOMATO, I SAY TOMATO!

Where can you find English speakers? The answer is nearly everywhere in the world. English is an international language of business, science and technology. More than 80% of the information in the world's computers is in English. The main language used on the Internet is English. Also, English is an official or co-official language in more than 45 countries. These countries are in Africa, Asia, Europe, South America, the South Pacific, North America and the Caribbean Islands.

In many of these countries, people speak British English. For example, they speak British English in India, Jamaica, Kenya, Hong Kong and Fiji. British English is different from American English, so sometimes people don't understand each other very well. First, American English speakers use different words from British English speakers. In British English, a person takes a *lift* up to her *flat*. In the United States, a person takes an *elevator* up to her *apartment*. The spelling of some words is also different. For instance, the American English word "color" is spelled "colour" in British English. In addition, people speak English with many different accents using different intonation.

However, English does not have the most speakers in the world. Many, many more people speak Mandarin Chinese than English!

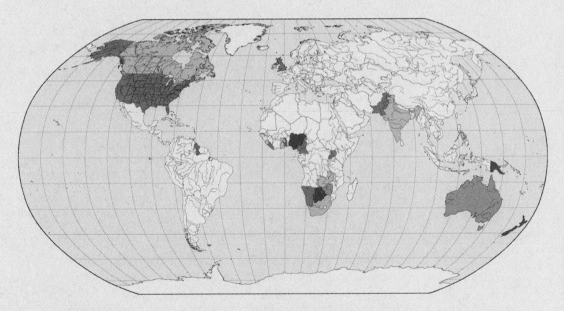

Shaded countries have English as their official language

B. Expressions of Fact

Readings are organized in different ways. Sometimes, a reading is organized by time. For example, a story like "A Passion for English" is organized by time. "You Say Tomato, I Say Tomato" is organized by related facts. Some expressions used in this kind of reading are: *also, in addition, however, another* and *for example*.

Look at the expressions in the box below. Find and underline them in the text. Think about what the words mean. Then answer the questions below.

however	also	in addition	for example

1. Which word or expression can you use to give an example?

   a. Also

   b. For example

   c. First

2. Which TWO words or expressions can you use to give more information?

   a. Also

   b. However

   c. In addition

3. Which word can you use to give a contrasting idea?

   a. However

   b. Also

   c. In addition

Circle the expressions in the paragraph below to complete the sentences.

COMING TO AMERICA
The United States is a country of immigrants and refugees. From 1820 to 1914 more than 33 million came to the United States from all over the world. From 1941 to 1987 about 14 million people legally immigrated. People continue to come today. They come for many different reasons.
<u>Also/ For example</u>, they come for new opportunities in jobs and education. <u>In addition/ However</u>, they come to escape war. <u>Also/ For example,</u> people come for religious freedom. <u>Also/ However</u>, in recent years, it is more difficult for people to come to the U.S.

COMMUNICATING YOUR IDEAS

A. Talk About It

Work in a small group. Answer the questions.

1. What language(s) do you speak? What other language(s) do you want to learn?

2. Are you an immigrant, refugee, international student?

3. Did you study English in your native country? If yes, did you learn British or American English? How did you feel in your English classes?

4. Do you try to speak only English in class? at work? at home?

5. What do you do to practice English outside of class?

6. What advice would you give to someone who is afraid to speak English?

7. What English-speaking countries would you like to visit?

8. Do you want your children to be bilingual or multinational? Explain.

9. What is your plan for learning English?

B. Write About It

Write a paragraph about your experiences learning English. Use Marit's story in Part One to help you. Don't forget to use simple past verb forms (see p. 129).

BONJOUR!

PRE-READING

Look at the picture of Patty. Where is she? What's she doing? Is she happy? Read the email she sent to her parents and find out if you're right.

| To: | Mom and Dad |
| Subject: | Bonjour! |

Send | Save | Print | Forward   ☰ ☰ ☰   **B** *I* U

Bonjour! I am having a good time in France, but French is not easy! I can't speak very well. When people talk to me in French, I can't understand them. I have to say "What?" about three times before I can understand them. I feel so stupid sometimes. When I try to answer, I get shy and I am afraid to say anything. Sometimes I am tongue-tied and can't speak.

At school, we have to write a journal in French about our experiences here. I'm good at grammar, I guess. I know most of the verb tenses, and I can express myself on paper. Writing is easier than speaking and listening for me.

My French is improving. I want to make it even better as soon as possible. My goal is to be able to speak with French people easily.

continued →

I would like to get a job where I can speak French with French people. This would really help me. Right now, I can't understand very much French TV, either. Everyone speaks so quickly! Another one of my goals is to understand French television and movies. I am reading French newspapers too, but there is so much new vocabulary.

Well, I'm glad I'm here in Paris. I am visiting a lot of great places. On Saturday, I went to the top of the Eiffel Tower. It was beautiful!

Je t'aime! (which means "I love you' in French).

Patty

READING AND WORD STUDY SKILLS

A. Understanding the Main Ideas

Read the sentences below. Put a check (✓) next to the correct sentences. Put a cross (X) next to the incorrect sentences.

1. __X__ Patty is comfortable speaking French with people.

2. _____ Patty is comfortable writing in French.

3. _____ Patty wants to listen to French radio.

4. _____ Patty is learning a lot of French.

5. _____ Patty is sad in Paris. She wants to go home.

B. Finding Details

Draw a line to complete the sentences.

1. Patty often asks people   French TV very well.

2. Patty writes in a   journal.

3. Patty reads   to repeat.

4. Patty can't understand   the top of the Eiffel Tower.

5. Patty went to   French newspapers.

C. Learning New Words

Read the sentences below. Guess the meaning of the word in bold. Do not use your dictionary! Circle the correct definition.

1. I get **shy** and I am afraid to say anything. **Shy** means

   a. not liking people
   b. not liking to talk to people
   c. happy to talk with people

2. Sometimes I am **tongue-tied** and can't speak. **Tongue-tied** means

   a. to be comfortable speaking
   b. to talk with a loud voice
   c. to have trouble speaking

3. I'm **good at** grammar, I guess. I know most of the verb tenses, and I can express myself on paper. I'm **good at** means

   a. I can't do it
   b. I can do it
   c. I don't like to

4. My French is **improving**. I want to make it even better as soon as possible. **Improving** means:

   a. not very good
   b. getting better
   c. staying the same

5. Well, I'm **glad** I'm here in Paris. I am visiting a lot of great places. **Glad** means

   a. unhappy
   b. happy
   c. tired

D. Using New Words

Now write your own sentences with the words in the box.

shy	tongue-tied	good at	improving	glad

1. _____

2. _____

OAKLAND COMMUNITY COLLEGE

To _Carmela_

Date _4/11_

I got these preview
copies (because I ordered
ESL materials for our SI).
Thought you may like
them. Enjoy!

LORI A. LINDEN
Faculty
Individualized Instruction Center
Southfield Campus

E-Mail: lalinden@oaklandcc.edu
Phone: 248.233.2738
Fax: 248.233.2828

3. _____

4. _____

5. _____

COMMUNICATING YOUR IDEAS

A. Talk About It

Look at "Bonjour!" again. Complete the chart about Patty. Then complete the chart about you and a classmate. Share your answers with your class.

	Patty	Me	My Partner
What are you good at?	grammar, writing		
What are you not good at?			
What are your goals?			

B. Interviewing

Interview someone studying a foreign language. Then report back to your class. Use these expressions to help you:

Starting: *Excuse me, can I ask you a few questions?*
Repeating: *Would you say that again, please?*
Ending: *Thanks so much for talking with me!*

1. What language are you learning?

2. Why are you studying it?

3. What special strategies do you use to learn it?

4. What are your strong and weak points in the language?

5. What would you like to do better in the language?

6. What are your goals for learning the language?

ONE STEP BEYOND

■ **Internet**
Find websites that will help you learn English. Share them with your classmates.

■ **More Readings**
If you want to read a story about an immigrant and English, go to the library to find "No Speak English" from *The House on Mango Street* by Sandra Cisneros. How does the woman in the story feel about coming to the U.S.? How does she feel about English?

■ **Movies**
Watch a movie such as *El Norte*, *Avalon* or *Green Card*. Why do the people in the movies want to learn English? What are their strategies and plans?

■ **Music**
Listen to the song *Let's Call The Whole Thing Off* by Cole Porter. Listen to the pronounciation of the words.

■ **At Your School**
Find out if your school has tutors, a Writing Center, a language laboratory, conversation partners or other resources to help you learn English.

■ **Journal**
Like Patty in Part 2, it's a good idea to keep a journal about your experiences. Write about why you want to learn English. Write about the plans and strategies you have for learning English. Use the examples from the unit.

■ **Vocabulary**
Start a vocabulary list of all of the new words you learn in each unit in this book. Write the lists in your journal.

■ **CNN®**
Remember to watch the CNN® video clip for this unit.

STORMY WEATHER

GETTING READY

Look at the pictures below. Answer the questions in groups.

1. What's happening in each picture?

2. Where do these weather events happen?

3. Can these weather events happen in the United States? Where?

THE TORNADO

PRE-READING

Predicting

To predict means to guess. When we predict, we think about what will happen. Predicting is a useful reading skill. Predicting shows you what to expect before you read. It also helps you to guess new vocabulary and read faster.

Look at the picture. Discuss the following questions in a small group.

1. What is happening to the house?

2. What is the boy doing? Why?

3. What will happen next?

THE TORNADO

One day, Billy was playing basketball in his friend's garage in Kokomo, Indiana. He was having a great time. Suddenly, it became dark. A very loud noise frightened him. He looked up and saw the sky was very gray. It became very windy, and without warning a gust of wind broke the garage into pieces. The pieces fell on top of Billy and cut his head. Then the wind picked the pieces up. It blew them all away.

continued →

Billy lay on the ground. He looked up and saw a big tornado. Things were flying around very fast in the tornado. Then the tornado picked up Billy. First, the tornado blew him into the roof of a neighbor's house. Billy screamed. Next, the tornado took Billy up and away again, and then it put him down very gently. Billy looked around for help. He saw a clothesline. He hugged the clothesline pole. He was holding the pole tightly, but the wind was too strong. The tornado pulled him off the pole and picked him up again.

Next, the tornado dropped Billy into a fishpond in a neighbor's backyard. Billy climbed out of the water. He was wet. Electric power lines were hanging down on the street. They were swinging and sparking. After that, Billy ran home as fast as he could.

Finally, Billy arrived at his house. He pulled on the back door, and the door broke. Billy was surprised because there was nothing in the house. It was empty. The tornado blew away the roof and all of the furniture. It even blew away the refrigerator! Billy was frightened and called out to his family.

His mom shouted, "We're here, Billy! We're okay! Thank goodness you're okay, too." They came running out of the basement and hugged him. Billy and his family were safe. The tornado destroyed their house but not their family.

READING AND WORD STUDY SKILLS

A. Understanding the Main Ideas

Put the sentences in the correct order.

1. _____ Billy ran home. His house was destroyed, but his family was safe.

2. _____ Billy hugged a clothesline pole tightly.

3. _____ The tornado blew Billy into the roof of a neighbor's house.

4. __1__ Billy was playing basketball in the garage.

5. _____ The tornado blew away the garage.

6. _____ It dropped Billy into a fishpond.

B. Finding Details

Read the following sentences. Circle T for true or F for false. Then correct the sentences that are wrong.

playing
1. Billy was ~~working~~ in the garage.   T   (F)

2. It became light.   T   F

3. The tornado was very quiet.   T   F

4. Something cut Billy's arm.   T   F

5. Electric power lines were hanging down.   T   F

6. The back door broke when Billy pulled it.   T   F

C. Drawing Conclusions

Drawing conclusions means to look at information and then guess about other things related to this. Many readings have information that is hidden or not stated clearly. We have to look at what is clear and guess about what is not clear in a reading. Circle the correct answer to complete each sentence.

1. It was
   a. night.
   b. day.

2. Billy hugged the pole because
   a. he was happy.
   b. he didn't want the tornado to pick him up again.

3. When Billy ran home
   a. he was wet.
   b. he was dry.

4. When the electrical wires were hanging down, Billy was
   a. safe.
   b. in danger.

5. The tornado blew away the refrigerator because
   a. it was strong.
   b. it was hungry.

D. Learning New Words

Complete the story with the correct words.

broke	blew	picked up	screamed	frightened

One day, Billy was playing basketball in the garage. A very loud noise

1) _____ him. It became very windy. A strong wind

2) _____ the garage into pieces.

　　Billy saw a big tornado. Things were flying around very fast in the tornado. Then the tornado 3) _____ Billy, and he was flying around, too! First, the tornado 4) _____ Billy into the roof of a neighbor's house. Billy 5) _____. Next, the tornado took Billy up and away again, and then it put him down very gently.

hugged	destroyed	tightly	dropped	safe

　　Billy looked around for help. He saw a clothesline. He

6) _____ the clothesline pole. He was holding the pole

7) _____, but the wind was too strong. It pulled him off the pole.

　　Next, the tornado 8) _____ Billy into a fishpond. Billy climbed out of the water. He was dripping wet. Electric power lines were hanging down on the street. Billy ran home as fast as he could.

　　Finally, Billy arrived at his house. There was nothing inside the house. Billy was frightened and called out to his family.

　　His mom shouted, "We're here, Billy! We're okay!" Billy and his family were 9) _____. The tornado 10) _____ their house but not their family.

E. Using New Words

Circle the correct word to complete each sentence.

1. The little boy _blew / dropped_ a glass of milk. The milk was all over the floor. The glass _broke / destroyed_.

2. The children built a sandcastle. Then the waves _picked up / destroyed_ it.

3. His grandmother was so happy. She _hugged / broke_ him.

4. My sister is _frightened / gently_ of spiders. Last night she _blew / screamed_ when she saw a spider.

5. The little girl held her mother's hand _tightly / gently_ at the busy market.

6. The wind _destroyed / blew_ my hat off.

7. I _picked up / dropped_ my baby and hugged her.

8. We have a security guard at work. He makes me feel _frightened / safe_.

F. Compound Nouns

Compound words are two nouns put together. They make one new word. Understanding how compound nouns are formed can help you learn more vocabulary.

Example: _book + store = bookstore_

1. Draw a line to match a word on the left with one on the right to make a compound noun.

1. hair	a. work
2. back	b. dresser
3. fire	c. yard
4. rain	d. fighter
5. home	e. ball
6. foot	f. bow

2. Look back at the story "The Tornado" in this chapter. Find four compound words.

3. Write a list of other compound nouns with your class.

COMMUNICATING YOUR IDEAS

A. Roleplaying

1. If you could interview Billy, his mother or father, what questions would you ask? Write them below.

    Example: *Did you go to the hospital, Billy?*

    1. _____

    2. _____

    3. _____

    4. _____

2. Get into a group of three students. One student is the interviewer, one is Billy and one is Billy's mother or father. The interviewer can use the questions from above to make an interview.

B. Write About It

1. Readings are organized in different ways. Sometimes a reading is organized as a list of facts, such as "I Say Tomato" from Unit 1. "The Tornado" is a story. Stories are organized by time. Some examples of words used to show time are: *first, later, soon, before, while* and *then*.

    Look back at "The Tornado." Circle the words the author uses to show time:

    Examples: *One day, first*

2. Did you or someone you know ever see a tornado? Were you ever in a bad rainstorm or snowstorm? What did you do? How did you feel? Write a story about extreme weather. Use some of the time words from "The Tornado." Share your story in class. Don't forget to use past simple and past progressive verb forms (see Appendix p. xx).

THE HOTTEST PLACE IN THE WORLD

PRE-READING

Look at the map. Read the information in the boxes. Match each box with the numbers on the map.

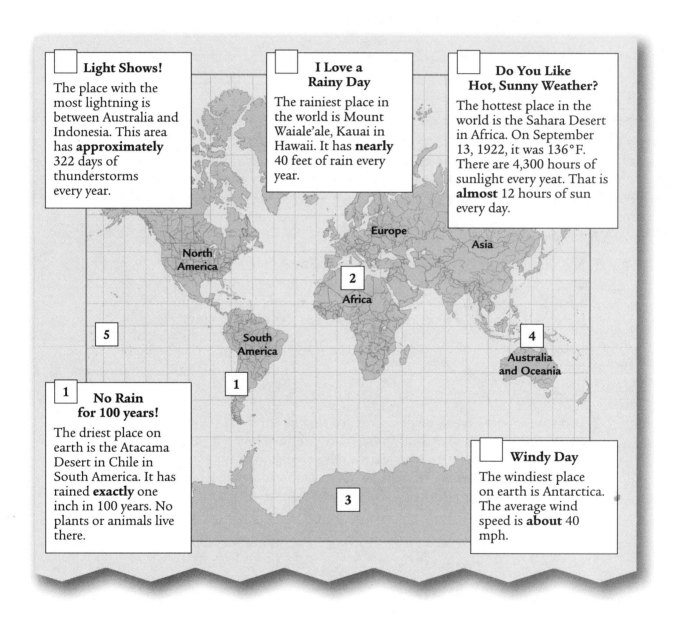

Light Shows!

The place with the most lightning is between Australia and Indonesia. This area has **approximately** 322 days of thunderstorms every year.

I Love a Rainy Day

The rainiest place in the world is Mount Waiale'ale, Kauai in Hawaii. It has **nearly** 40 feet of rain every year.

Do You Like Hot, Sunny Weather?

The hottest place in the world is the Sahara Desert in Africa. On September 13, 1922, it was 136°F. There are 4,300 hours of sunlight every yeat. That is **almost** 12 hours of sun every day.

No Rain for 100 years!

The driest place on earth is the Atacama Desert in Chile in South America. It has rained **exactly** one inch in 100 years. No plants or animals live there.

Windy Day

The windiest place on earth is Antarctica. The average wind speed is **about** 40 mph.

READING AND WORD STUDY SKILLS

A. Finding Details

Complete the chart with information from the map.

Place	Record	How much
	the driest place	1 inch of rain in 100 years
Sahara Desert		40 feet of rain every year
		average 40 mph wind
	the most lightning	

B. Learning New Words

Circle the different word in each list. Use your dictionary to help.

1. nearly, almost, (never)
2. almost, approximately, exactly
3. nearly, average, almost
4. exactly, about, nearly
5. approximately, nearly, exactly
6. never, nearly, about

C. Using New Words

Write four sentences about the weather in your native country. Use *nearly, approximately, about* and *almost.* Discuss them in class.

Example: *In Santa Barbara, it is hot nearly every day.*

1. _____

2. _____

3. _____

4. _____

SKILL BUILDER

D. Using Adjectives with –y

An adjective is a word that describes a noun. Many nouns can be changed into adjectives by adding –y to the end of the word. Look at page 145 for information on adjectives.

1. Write adjectives for the nouns below.

a. wind_____*windy*_____   f. cloud_____

b. fog_____   g. breeze_____

c. smog_____   h. shower_____

d. sun_____   i. snow_____

e. sun_____

2. Look at the weather map on page 27. Write five sentences describing the weather in the cities on the map.

Example: *It's sunny and cold in Chicago today.*

a. _____

b. _____

c. _____

d. _____

e. _____

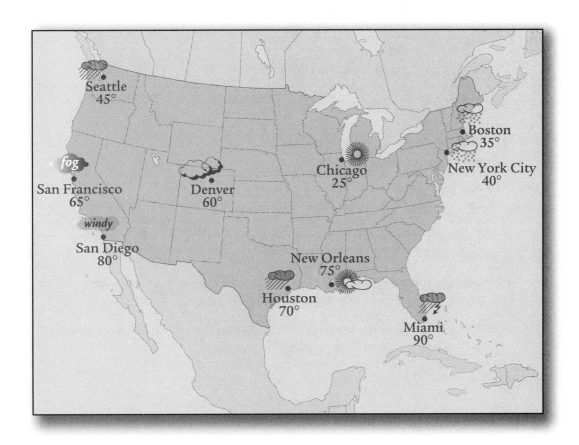

COMMUNICATING YOUR IDEAS

A. Talk About It

Look again at the weather map. Talk in pairs about the weather.

Example: *Q: What's the weather like in Boston?*
            A: It's cold and snowy today.

B. Talk About It

Work in a small group. Discuss the questions.

1. Have you or someone you know experienced stormy weather? Describe it.

2. The tornado in the story happened in Indiana. What extreme weather events happen where you live?

3. What can you do if a tornado or other bad weather happens where you live?

4. What's the weather like today where you live? What will it be like tomorrow?

5. What are the names of the four seasons in English? What is the weather like during each season where you live?

6. What is your favorite season? What is your favorite kind of weather? Why? What do you like to do in this weather?

GATHERING LEAVES

PRE-READING

1. Look at the picture. What time of year is it? What are the people doing? How do they feel?

2. Read the following excerpt from a poem by the famous American poet Robert Frost. This poem is about leaves in the fall. Think about the sounds and meaning of the words.

GATHERING LEAVES

Spades take up leaves
No better than spoons,
And bags full of leaves
Are light as balloons.

I make a great noise
Of rustling all day
Like rabbit and deer
Running away.

But the mountains I raise
Elude my embrace,
Flowing over my arms
And into my face.

spades—small tools used for digging
rustling—a soft sound made from brushing
raise—build
elude—escape capture
embrace—hug
flowing—moving smoothly and easily

READING AND WORD STUDY SKILLS

A. Understanding the Main Ideas

Complete the following sentences.

1. The spades are not good for picking up leaves. The spades are like

   _____.

2. The bags are full of leaves. The bags are light

   like _____.

3. The noise of the leaves is like _____.

4. There are many leaves. They are like a_____.

5. What happens when he tries to pick up the leaves with his arms?

   _____

6. Does he like the leaves? _____

B. Rhyming Words

Words **rhyme** when they sound similar. In the poem *Gathering Leaves,* the poet Robert Frost uses rhymes. These pairs of words rhyme.

   Example: *blue—zoo   red—bed   fat—cat   school—pool*

Look at the poem again. Look at the last word in each line. Answer the questions.

1. What rhymes with **spoons**? _____

2. What rhymes with **day**? _____

3. What rhymes with **embrace**? _____

4. Can you think of other words that rhyme? Write some with your class.

Read the poem out loud again. Listen to the musical rhythm and rhymes.

COMMUNICATING YOUR IDEAS

A. Talk About It

What is your favorite season? Assign a season to each of the four corners of your classroom. Go to the corner of the season you like best. Tell the other students in that corner why you like that season best. As a group, report back to the class.

B. Write About It

What is your favorite season or kind of weather? Why? Write about it. Share your ideas with your group.

> Example: *I like snow at night. I like it when there is no wind and the snow falls silently. I like to walk when there is fresh snow. It is so quiet and beautiful. I can feel the cold air on my face. The lights make pretty reflections on the snow.*

C. Writing a Poem

Write a short poem about the summer. Try to include words that rhyme. Here are some rhyming words to get you started:

sun—fun	wave—gave	sea—free	sand—hand
pool—cool	tan—man	play—day	light—bright

■ **Internet, Television or Newspaper**
Look for the weather forecast for your area. Find the weather forecast in your native country. Note down in your journal the weather for today and tomorrow.

■ **Movies**
Watch part of a movie or documentary about extreme weather. Some possible movies are *The Wizard of Oz, The Perfect Storm, Twister* and *Alive*. In your journal, write about the kind of weather there is in the movie and the problems it caused.

■ **Music**
Listen to a song and find the rhymes. Some possible songs are *It's a Rainy Night in Georgia, Raindrops Keep Falling on My Head*, or *Singing in the Rain*.

■ **More Readings**
Read *The North Wind and the Sun* from Aesop's Fables or another fable about weather events. Retell the story or act out the story for your class.

■ **Journal**
Write down your thoughts about this unit. What did you like? What did you learn? What surprised you?

■ **Vocabulary**
Copy the words from this unit in to your vocabulary log.

■ **CNN.**®
Remember to watch the CNN® video clip for this unit.

OUT OF AFRICA

GETTING READY

What do you know about Africa? Work with your group. Circle the correct answers. Then check your answers in the Appendix (page xx).

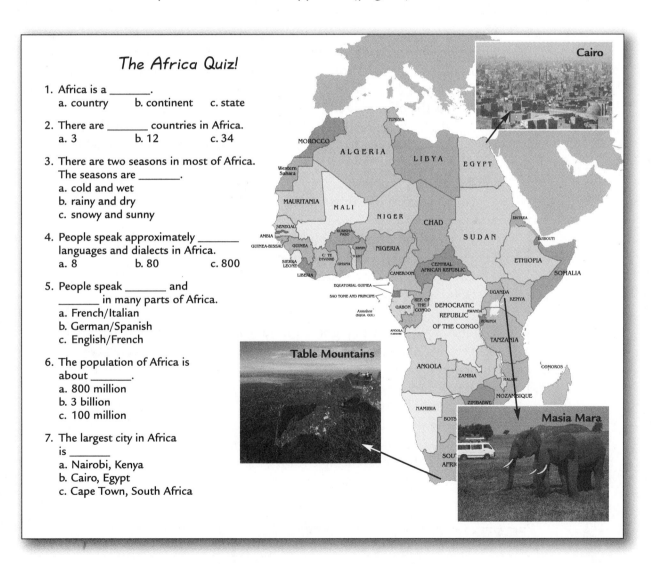

The Africa Quiz!

1. Africa is a _____.
   a. country   b. continent   c. state

2. There are _____ countries in Africa.
   a. 3   b. 12   c. 34

3. There are two seasons in most of Africa.
   The seasons are _____.
   a. cold and wet
   b. rainy and dry
   c. snowy and sunny

4. People speak approximately _____
   languages and dialects in Africa.
   a. 8   b. 80   c. 800

5. People speak _____ and
   _____ in many parts of Africa.
   a. French/Italian
   b. German/Spanish
   c. English/French

6. The population of Africa is
   about _____.
   a. 800 million
   b. 3 billion
   c. 100 million

7. The largest city in Africa
   is _____
   a. Nairobi, Kenya
   b. Cairo, Egypt
   c. Cape Town, South Africa

Cairo

Table Mountains

Masia Mara

A SPECIAL DELIVERY

PRE-READING

What is the title of this story? What is happening in the picture? What do you think the story is about? Why? Discuss in pairs.

A SPECIAL DELIVERY

Suzy and Spud lived in California with their five daughters. Spud liked traveling, so one summer, he went to Africa on a trip. He went on a safari to see wild animals. Suzy stayed home with the children.

Spud and his friends owned a big toy company. People who worked at the company liked to play jokes on each other.

Spud's friends wanted to play a joke on Spud and Suzy while Spud was in Africa, so one day, they sent a special letter to Suzy. It said,

Dear Suzy,
I'm having a great time here in Africa. There are many wild animals.

I'm sending a special souvenir to you. I hope you enjoy it. Please take good care of it until I get home.

Love to you and the girls,
Spud

On the same day, Suzy got a phone call. The caller told her that a delivery was coming in the afternoon. At one o'clock, a delivery truck stopped in front of Suzy's house. The deliveryman opened the back of the truck and gave Suzy a rope.

An animal was tied to the rope. This animal was big and heavy. It had a long trunk and big ears. "Oh, my gosh!" Suzy said. The animal was a baby elephant! The elephant ran out of the truck and into Suzy's yard. It began eating the bushes.

continued →

The deliveryman drove away in the truck. Suzy stood in the yard, holding the rope to the baby elephant. She asked, "What do I feed an elephant? Lettuce?" She laughed.

A few minutes later, a police officer came to talk to Suzy. He said, "It's illegal to have a wild animal here." He gave Suzy a ticket.

Spud's friends, who were hiding in the neighbor's backyard, were laughing. They had planned everything perfectly. They rented the elephant from a local petting zoo. They also asked the police officer to write the ticket! Spud's friends watched and filmed everything. They wanted Spud to see their joke when he came back from Africa.

Suzy gave a "thumbs up" to Spud's friends. What will the next joke be?

READING AND WORD STUDY SKILLS

A. Understanding the Main Ideas

1. Circle the other possible title for the story.

   a. Going on Safari

   b. A 750-pound Joke

   c. An Animal

2. Put the sentences into the correct order.

a. _____ A delivery truck delivered the souvenir to Suzy. It contained an elephant.

b. _____ Spud went on safari in Africa, and his family stayed home in California.

c. _____ The special message asked Suzy to take care of a souvenir.

d. _____ Suzy laughed about the joke and Spud's friends filmed everything for Spud to see.

e. _____ Spud's friends sent a special message to his wife Suzy as a joke.

B. Finding Details

Circle the correct answer.

1. The baby elephant came from _____.

   a. Africa   b. the petting zoo   c. Asia

2. The elephant was big and _____.

   a. light   b. heavy   c. long

3. The elephant walked in _____.

   a. the house   b. the road   c. the yard

4. When Suzy saw the elephant, she _____.

   a. cried   b. laughed   c. screamed

5. Spud's friends were hiding in _____.

   a. a neighbor's yard   b. a car   c. the delivery truck

C. Learning New Words

1. Look at the words in the box below. They all come from the story. Do you know what they mean? Put a check (✓) next to the words you think you know. Put a cross (X) next to the words you don't know. Put a question mark (?) next to the words you're not sure about.

rope	owned	illegal
souvenir	take care of	special
hiding	wild	laughed

2. Find the words in the story and underline them. Can you guess the meaning of the words you did not know? Look up any words you still don't know in your *Newbury House Dictionary of American English*.

3. Read the *Newbury House Dictionary for American English* dictionary definition for *joke*.

> **joke** /dʒoʊk/ *n.* **1** a funny idea or story with a surprise ending: *He has a great sense of humor and loves to tell jokes.* **2 to play a joke on s.o.:** to trick, (*syn.*) to play a prank: *His friends played a joke on him by sewing his pant legs together.* **3** a ridiculous situation: *That salary increase was so small that it was a joke!*
> —*v.* [I] **joked, joking, jokes 1** to tell a joke: *When she gets together with her friends, they joke a lot.* **2** to act playfully: *They dance and sing and joke around together.* -*adv.* **jokingly.**

a. Read the sentence below. Underline the correct definition from the dictionary.

"People who worked at the college liked to play jokes on each other."

b. Your dictionary tells you how to pronounce, or say, words properly. Find and circle /dʒoʊk/. Find the pronunciation guide at the back of your dictionary. Practice saying the word "joke."

c. Did Suzy's friends tell her a joke or play a joke on her?

D. Using New Words

Complete each sentence.

1. My uncle tells very funny _____.

2. A tiger is a _____ animal.

3. We _____ during the movie because it was funny.

4. The children were _____ under the table.

5. It is _____ to drink and drive.

6. The neighbors _____ a big truck, but they sold it.

7. My friend always brings me a _____ when she returns

   from a trip.

8. It is important to _____ your pets. They are very

   _____ animals.

Work with a partner. Complete the chart with the words in exercise D.
(Look at page 129 for information on verbs and adjectives.)

Noun	Verb	Adjective
1.	1.	1.
2.	2.	2.
	3.	3.
	4.	

E. Irregular Past Tense Verbs

1. In English, there are regular and irregular verbs in the past tense.
   Regular verbs use –ed at the end of the verb. Irregular verbs use many
   forms (see page 129 for more information).

2. Complete the table below with the correct past tense verb.

Base	Simple Past
go	went
think	_____
see	_____
have	_____
feel	_____
give	_____
sit	_____
send	_____

3. Look back at "The Tornado" story. Underline all the irregular past simple verbs.

4. Write five sentences using the irregular past tense verbs above.

a. _____

b. _____

c. _____

d. _____

e. _____

COMMUNICATING YOUR IDEAS

A. Role Playing

Work with a group or with your class. Act out the story of *A Special Delivery*. Take the parts of Suzy, the caller, the deliveryman, the policeman, the neighbors, Spud's friends and the baby elephant. What do you think each person will say and do?

MASAI MARA

SKILL BUILDER

PRE-READING

Scanning

1. Scanning means to read something very quickly. We don't read every word when we scan. Instead, we look only for specific information. Scan the web site. How many animals can you underline in 30 seconds?

Address: `http://www.lionkingstours.net`

KENYA
Eldoret
Kisumu
Nairobi

Prices

Reservations

More Information

MASAI MARA

An Unbelievable Adventure

Let Lion Kings Tours take you to the Masai Mara, Kenya's most popular game reserve!

Ride in our safari vans with our friendly guides to see Kenya's amazing wildlife. The big attraction is the Big Five: leopards, lions, buffalo, rhinos and elephants. You will also see many other rare animals and colorful birds. Many of these animals are endangered and rarely seen outside of Masai Mara.

One-day, two-day and three-day packages including hotel and all meals are available. Click on the links on the left for reservations and more information.

At Lion Kings Tours, we guarantee you will have an unforgettable safari.

READING AND WORD STUDY SKILLS

A. Understanding the Main Ideas

Check (✔) the sentences that are true. Put a cross (X) next to the sentences that are false. Correct the false sentences.

1. _____ Masai Mara is in Kenya.

2. _____ Kenya has many wild animals.

3. _____ The Big Five are the elephant, the hippo, the giraffe, the lion and the buffalo.

4. _____ Many animals in the Masai Mara game park are endangered species.

5. _____ Packages do not include hotel and meals.

6. _____ You cannot make reservations online.

7. _____ You can find the cost of the tours by clicking on the Prices link.

B. Learning New Words

1. Draw a line to match the adjective with the noun.

Adjectives	Nouns
1. friendly	a. game reserve
2. colorful	b. animals
3. rare	c. guides
4. unforgettable	d. birds
5. popular	e. safari

2. Fill in the gaps below with the right adjective. Guess first. Then check in your dictionary.

a. _____ memorable, wonderful

b. _____ helpful and pleasant

c. _____ not often heard or seen

d. _____ liked by many people

e. _____ having bright colors

C. Antonyms

1. Antonyms are opposite words. *Cold* and *hot* are opposites. *Dark* and *light* are opposites. Antonyms are often adjectives. Learning antonyms will help you know more words. Use your dictionary to find the opposites of the words below.

_____ strong		a. tiny
_____ loud		b. weak
_____ heavy		c. sit
_____ long		d. blunt
_____ sharp		e. close
_____ stand		f. quiet
_____ ask		g. short
_____ huge		h. answer
_____ popular		i. light
_____ give		j. receive
_____ open		k. unpopular
_____ rare		l. common

2. Circle the correct words to complete the sentences.

   a. Elephants are <u>big/small</u> and <u>heavy/light</u>. They have <u>long/short</u> trunks. They are very <u>strong/weak</u>.

   b. I always <u>give/receive</u> a birthday card from my grandmother on my birthday.

   c. When it rains, I <u>open/close</u> my window.

   d. A lizard is a <u>loud/quiet</u> animal with a <u>short/long</u> tail.

   e. When the telephone rings, I <u>ask/answer</u> it.

   f. Dinner is ready. Please <u>sit/stand</u> down.

   g. Many people stood in line to buy tickets to see the <u>popular/unpopular</u> singer.

   h. A knife is <u>blunt/sharp</u>.

   i. It is <u>rare/common</u> to see endangered animals in New York.

3. Write sentences about animals using the words above.

   Example: *A cheetah is fast. He isn't slow.*

COMMUNICATING YOUR IDEAS

A. Talk About It

Discuss these questions in groups.

1. Do you like to travel? Which countries have you been to?

2. Where would you like to travel? Why?

3. Would you like to go on a safari in Africa?

4. Did you ever see animals from Africa at a zoo? If yes, which ones did you see?

B. Write About It

1. Read the descriptions of the animals. Guess which animals they are.

a. This rare animal lives in Africa and Asia. It has very big feet and huge ears. It is gray. It has short hair and a short tail. It has a trunk. What is it?

b. This amazing animal lives in Africa. It hunts at night. It has sharp teeth and a long mane. What is it?

c. This animal lives in Africa and Asia. It is very heavy and slow. It has a sharp horn. It is not very colorful. It likes to eat grass. What is it?

2. Underline all the adjectives in the descriptions.

3. Write a description of an animal. Read your description to your group or to your class. Use some of the adjectives from the descriptions above. Your classmates will guess what animal you are describing.

APRIL FOOLS

PRE-READING

Fernanda is visiting her sister, who lives in Cape Town, South Africa. Fernanda sends an email to her best friend Mi-ra in the U.S. Look at the photos she sent. What did she see and do? Read the email to find out what happened.

READING AND WORD STUDY SKILLS

A. Understanding the Main Ideas

Circle the correct answer. Underline where you found your answers in the email.

1. Fernanda is visiting

    a. Mi-ra.
    b. her sister.
    c. no one.

2. Fernanda is spending a lot of time

    a. Eating breakfast.
    b. On the beach.
    c. Telling jokes.

3. Tomorrow, Fernanda is going to

    a. Company Gardens.
    b. shopping.
    c. Robben Island.

4. Fernand's sister is

    a. getting married.
    b. joking about getting married.
    c. has a secret.

| To: | Mi-ra |

| Subject: | Greetings from Cape Town! |

Send | Save | Print | Forward   ≡ ≡ ≡   **B** *I* <u>U</u>

Hi Mi-ra! How are you? How's your spring going? Are you having fun? I'm here in Cape Town visiting my sister. She's at college here with her boyfriend, Robert. Cape Town is a great city. There's a lot to see and do. It's very hot and sunny here. We're spending a lot of time on the beach. Yesterday we went to a place called Company Gardens to watch South African jazz bands. Tomorrow we are going to Robben Island. It's the place where Nelson Mandela was in prison. My guidebook says it is "a place forever connected with the fight for freedom."

Did you remember it's April Fools Day today? My sister loves playing jokes. At breakfast, she said, "Robert and I are going to elope! We're going to quit college and have children." I was so surprised! And then she said "April Fools! Just kidding!" Then I went into my bedroom and saw a big, ugly spider on the floor. I walked closer. The spider was fake!

So if you receive a phone call today about winning the lottery or something, don't get excited. It's probably an April Fools joke!

See you soon,
Fernanda

B. Finding Details

What are two practical jokes Fernanda writes about in her email?

1. _____

2. _____

C. Learning New Words

Unscramble the words below from Fernanda's letter. Then draw a line from the word to the correct definition.

1. eople_____   a. to leave
2. uitq_____   b. not real, a copy
3. kefa_____   c. to get married in secret

D. Using New Words

Write three sentences using the words from exercise C.

1. _____

2. _____

3. _____

COMMUNICATING YOUR IDEAS

A. Talk about It

Discuss the questions with a small group.

1. Do you have a holiday similar to April Fools Day in your native country?

2. Did you ever play a joke on someone, or did someone play a joke on you? Explain.

3. Did you like to play games when you were a child? Tell about one. Do you like to tell jokes? Tell one.

B. Talk about It

1. English has many expressions called idioms. Idioms are expressions made up of a few words. An idiom says one thing but means something else. Work with a partner. What do the idioms below mean? Match the sentences with the same meaning.

   1. _____ He's *the cat's meow.*   a. It's pouring outside.

   2. _____ He's *chicken.*   b. She does not feel comfortable here.

   3. _____ It's *raining cats and*   c. He's wonderful.
              dogs.
                                           d. He's afraid

   4. _____ She's *a fish out of*
              water.

2. Draw a picture representing one of these idioms to share with the class.

3. There are many more popular animal idioms. Interview a native speaker to find a few more.

■ **Internet or Library**

Go to the Internet or to a library and search for information about an animal. Find answers to the questions below. Prepare a short presentation to tell your class what you learned. Use pictures, charts or websites in your presentation.

1. What is the name of the animal?_____
2. Describe the animal. What does it look like?
3. Where does this animal live?
4. What does this animal like to eat?
5. What is the average life span of this animal? (How long does it usually live?)
6. How many offspring (babies) does this animal usually have?
7. Is this animal dangerous to humans? If yes, why?
8. Is this animal a source of food for people? (Do people eat it?)
9. Is this animal an endangered species? If yes, explain why.
10. Can this animal be a pet? If yes, would you like to have one in your home?
11. Tell some other interesting facts you learned about this animal.

■ **More Readings**

Visit your local library to find books and articles on Africa. Share information that you learn with your class.

■ **Movies**

Watch the following movies about Africa: *Out of Africa, I Dreamed of Africa, African Queen*. Write in your journals about the animals that you saw.

■ **In Your Community.**

Plan a trip to the zoo, an animal shelter or an animal rescue organization in your area. Learn more about what you can do to help animals.

■ **Journal**

Write about some of the questions from the "Talk About It" sections in Parts 2 and 3.

■ **Vocabulary**

Write all of the new words you learned in this unit. Include their parts of speech.

■ **CNN**®

Remember to watch the CNN® video clip for this unit.

EDUCATION FOR ALL

GETTING READY

1. Look at the pictures. Work in pairs. What's she doing? Is she busy?

2. Interview a partner. Ask the questions below. Write notes.

	Me	My Partner
1. Do you work? Full-time or part-time?		
2. How often do you come to school or college?		
3. Do you have to look after a family?		
4. Do you have much time to be by yourself?		

HOW THRIFT TURNED TO GIFT

PRE-READING

1. Look up the word *thrift* in your Dictionary and complete the definition.

   thrift spending _____ carefully.

2. Work with a group. Look at the statements below. Check the things that are important for someone who wants to be thrifty. Report back to your class.

   a. _____ shop at sales
   b. _____ give money to charity
   c. _____ take taxis
   d. _____ work two jobs

   e. _____ save money in a bank
   f. _____ eat at home, not at restaurants
   g. _____ use credit cards
   h. _____ compare prices

3. Look at the photo of Oseola McCarty. She was a thrifty woman. What things do you think she did from the list above? How do you think she made a living? Read the story and find out how this woman's thrift and hard work turned into a gift for others.

HOW THRIFT TURNED TO GIFT

Oseola McCarty was born in 1908 in Mississippi. She lived with her grandmother, mother and aunt. They grew corn, sugar cane, peas, watermelon and potatoes. They also did laundry by hand for people. They washed the clothes in a big pot of boiling water in their backyard. Then they hung them outside to dry in the sun. Finally, they ironed the clothes.

Young Oseola loved going to school, but she dropped out of school when she was twelve years old. She took care of her aunt because her aunt was sick. Oseola also continued to wash and iron clothes for people. Soon Miss McCarty began to pay the water, electricity and gas

continued →

---

bills for her family. She paid for groceries and other things, too. She gave money to her church, and every month, she put some money in the bank.

Miss McCarty worked for many years, because she loved working. Sometimes she got extra jobs on her days off. She never bought a car. She didn't spend money on transportation. She always walked. She was thrifty. Finally, when Miss McCarty was eighty-six years old, she stopped working.

One day when she went to the bank, the bank officer asked her a question. He said, "What do you want to do with all of your money?" She was amazed. Over the years, she saved a lot of money! So she gave some money to her church, and she gave some money to her cousins. Finally, she gave some money to make her dream come true.

Her dream was to help children go to college. She wanted to help African-American families who couldn't afford to send their children to college. So she gave most of her money to the University of Southern Mississippi for scholarships. Miss McCarty gave $150,000. She said, "I'm giving it away so that the children won't have to work so hard, like I did."

A young woman named Stephanie Bullock was the first student to receive the Oseola McCarty Scholarship. One day, Stephanie visited Miss McCarty. Stephanie ran to her and said, "Thank you for helping me go to college. Thank you for the scholarship. It helped me so much." Miss McCarty smiled and felt so proud. She wants to see Stephanie and other students graduate from college.

Many people were inspired by Miss McCarty's giving. More than 600 people gave $330,000 more to Oseola McCarty's special scholarship fund. Many more young people now have an opportunity to go to college, thanks to Oseola McCarty's dream.

READING AND WORD STUDY SKILLS

A. Understanding the Main Ideas

Circle the other possible title for the story.

1. From Savings to Scholarships

2. Washing Clothes

3. College and Scholarships

4. School Drop Out

B. Finding Details

Draw a line to complete the sentences from the reading.

1. Young Oseola dropped out of school	a. when she was 86 years old.
2. She stopped working	b. when she went to the bank.
3. The bank officer asker her a question	c. when she hear about Miss McCarty.
4. Many people were inspired by Miss McCarty's giving	d. when she was 12 years old.

C. Learning New Words

Match the underlined words with the correct definition.

---
a. to quit, to leave or stop participating in
b. an award to help pay school tuition
c. chances to do something new and better
d. to get something from someone
e. to be able to pay for something without difficulty
---

1. _____ Learning English will give me new *opportunities*.

2. _____ Rodrigo needed a *scholarship* to go to college because his family didn't have enough money to help him.

3. _____ Some people *drop out* of school.

4. _____ We wanted to buy the car, but we couldn't _afford_ it. It was too expensive.

5. _____ I _received_ a birthday present from my girlfriend.

> f. to finish school with a diploma, degree or certificate
> g. to imagine or hope for
> h. very surprised
> i. caused to work hard, motivate
> j. careful with money

6. _____ Sometimes school is difficult for me, but I want to _graduate_.

7. _____ My grandmother is a hardworking, intelligent woman. I really admire her. She _inspired_ me to follow my dreams.

8. _____ My aunt Lizzie always uses coupons and compares prices. She is _thrifty_.

9. _____ My brother _dreams_ of being a jet pilot.

10. _____ My friends were _amazed_ when I shaved my head.

D. Using New Words

Write your own sentences using some of the words from above. Choose the words you found most difficult.

1. _____

2. _____

3. _____

4. _____

5. _____

6. _____

E. Drawing Conclusions

Circle T for true, F for false or ITK for impossible to know.

1. Miss McCarty spent a lot of money on herself.   T   F   ITK

2. Miss McCarty was poor when she was a child.   T   F   ITK

3. Miss McCarty had 3 brothers and 4 sisters.   T   F   ITK

4. Miss McCarty was sad when she dropped out
   of school.   T   F   ITK

5. Miss McCarty was careful with her money.   T   F   ITK

6. Miss McCarty was generous.   T   F   ITK

F. Word Webs

It is useful to link new words to other words. Making a "word web" can help you remember new words. Complete the word web using the words in the box. Then add words of your own.

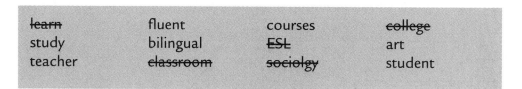

learn	fluent	courses	college
study	bilingual	ESL	art
teacher	classroom	sociolgy	student

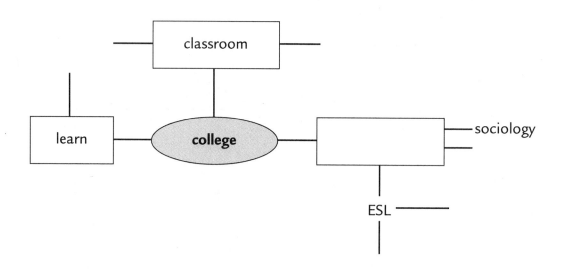

COMMUNICATING YOUR IDEAS

A. Talk About It

Work in a small group. Discuss the questions below.

1. Who inspires you?

2. What is something you can't afford but would like to buy?

3. Do you or someone you know make something by hand?

4. What is something you are proud of?

5. What kind of new opportunities will you have when you learn English well? Give examples.

6. What do you want to do after you graduate?

7. What's your dream?

B. Role Playing

Work with a partner. Look back at the words in exercise C. Choose four words. Write a dialogue between Miss McCarty and Stephanie. Include the four words you chose. Then practice it and perform it for the class.

SCHOLARSHIPS PAY OFF

PRE-READING

Look at the newspaper article. What's the name of the newspaper? What is the title of the article? Look at the photo. What do you think the article is about?

READING AND WORD STUDY SKILLS

A. Identifying Main Ideas in a Paragraph

There are four paragraphs in the article. Paragraphs usually have one main idea. This idea gives you the most important information the writer wants to communicate. Skim (read quickly) the article. Which paragraph contains the following main ideas? Write the number of the paragraph next to its main idea.

1. _____ There are many strange scholarships.

2. _____ All students can receive scholarships.

3. _____ Spending time trying to get scholarships is a good idea for any student.

4. _____ One student worked hard applying for scholarships and received a lot of money.

SCHOLARSHIPS PAY OFF

How tall are you? Are you a skateboarder? Do you like to knit? Whoever you are, whatever you do, there is a scholarship for you!

One student, Ryan, made it his job to get scholarships. He is the son of a farmer and needed more money to come to college. He started applying for scholarships when he was in high school. He received a big scholarship from the college because he is an excellent student. He also won a national competition and received a $5,000 award. Sometimes he worked very hard filling out applications and writing essays for scholarships, even for small amounts of money. By his junior year of college, he had received more than $61,000!

Sure, there are scholarships for good students like Ryan. There are scholarships for good athletes or for students in need. But what about the rest of us? In fact, there are some very surprising scholarships for everyone else. Believe it or not, there is a scholarship for skateboarders with a GPA of 2.5 or higher. These student skateboarders can receive $5,000 or $1,000 awards. There is also a scholarship for tall people. Women 5′10″ or taller and men 6′2″ or taller can apply. These tall students are eligible for $1,000 awards. Don't worry, short people, there is a scholarship for you if you are 4′10″ or shorter. You can get $1,000 too. A milk mustache scholarship goes to 25 students who are excellent students and athletes. They each get $7,500 and their pictures taken with a milk mustache! Finally, a wool competition awards $1,000 and $2,000 to students who knit wool clothes with excellent design and creativity.

So you don't have to be a straight A student to get a scholarship. One counselor in our Financial Aid Office says, "It takes time and effort to apply for scholarships, but it is worth it!"

Apply Now!

See your counselor about scholarship and financial aid opportunities.
Call extension 423 for an appointment.

B. Finding Details

Read paragraph three about unusual scholarships again. Complete the chart.

Type of scholarship	Who can apply	How much money
Skateboarding	students with a GPA of 2.5 or higher	$5,000 or $1,000

C. Learning New Words

Draw a line from the word or expression to its correct definition.

1. Applying   a. physical or mental work

2. Filling out   b. asking for admission

3. Effort   c. important enough to spend a lot of time and effort doing

4. Worth it   d. completing a form

D. Using New Words

Complete the sentences with the correct words.

effort	filling out	apply	worth it

1. I spent a lot of time studying for the test. It was _____ because I got an A in the class.

2. Robert is _____ an application for a new job.

3. My grandfather made a big _____ to visit me at Christmas. He came all the way from Mexico.

4. You can _____ for a loan at the bank to start a new business.

COMMUNICATING YOUR IDEAS

A. Talk About It

Discuss the questions with a small group. Then report back to your class.

1. Are you eligible for any of the scholarships in the article?

2. Is it expensive to go to college in your native country? In the USA?

3. Do you have financial aid, or do you have a scholarship now? Would you like to get financial aid or a scholarship in the future?

B. Role-playing

What is most important in giving scholarships? Work in a group. You are a committee deciding the most important things to consider in giving scholarships. As a group, rank the items below from most important (#1) to least important (#10). Then report back to your class.

_____ students who participate in sports

_____ students with good grades

_____ students who do community service

_____ full time students

_____ students who have leadership positions

_____ students with financial need

_____ minority students

_____ single parent students

_____ students with jobs

_____ other: _____

HAIRS

PRE-READING

1. Quickly scan the reading below about a writer named Sandra Cisneros. Circle T for true or F for false.

   a. She was born in 1945.   T   F

   b. She was born in Chicago.   T   F

   c. She visited Mexico one time.   T   F

   d. She writes poems.   T   F

   e. She received a scholarship.   T   F

SANDRA CISNEROS

(1954-) Sandra Cisneros is a popular poet and writer. She was born in 1954 in Chicago. She grew up with her working class parents and six brothers. Her mother was Mexican-American, and her father was from Mexico City. She visited Mexico often when she was growing up. Mexico was like a second home for her.

She received a scholarship to go to Loyola University in Chicago. She graduated in 1976. She got a graduate degree at the University of Iowa in 1978. Her first book, published in 1983, was called *The House on Mango Street*.

Sandra Cisneros writes about her experience living in two cultures. She writes in English, but everything she writes about comes from her experience growing up in a Spanish-speaking family. She writes about being bicultural and bilingual.

2. Scan the poem from Sandra Cisneros's book, *The House on Mango Street*.
   Circle the names of the five family members in the story.

HAIRS

Everybody in our family has different hair.
My Papa's hair is like a broom, all up in
the air. And me, my hair is lazy. It never
obeys barrettes or bands. Carlos's hair is
thick and straight. He doesn't need to
comb it. Nenny's hair is slippery—slides
out of your hand. And Kiki, who is the
youngest, has hair like fur.

But my mother's hair, my mother's
hair, like little rosettes, like little candy
circles all curly and pretty because she
pinned it in pincurls all day, sweet to
put your nose into when she is holding
you, holding you and you feel safe, is the
warm smell of bread before you bake it,
is the smell when she makes room for
you on her side of the bed still warm
with her skin, and you sleep near her,
the rain outside falling and Papa
snoring. The snoring, the rain and
Mama's hair that smells like bread.

READING AND WORD STUDY SKILLS

A. Understanding the Main Ideas

Read the summaries below. Which is the best summary?

1. _____ Sandra Cisneros is a poet who was born in Chicago in 1954.
   She had a big family with six brothers. They spoke Spanish at home.
   Her family was working class.

2. _____ Sandra Cisneros is a popular Latina writer. She grew up in the
   United States, but Mexico was also like a home to her. Her writing is
   about her experiences being bilingual and bicultural.

3. _____ Sandra Cisneros speaks English and Spanish. She writes about
   life around her. Her stories are published.

B. Learning New Words

Draw a line from a word to its definition.

1. fur		a.	a cleaning tool
2. obey		b.	the hairy coat of an animal
3. slippery		c.	to do what is asked
4. broom		d.	not liking and avoiding work
5. lazy		e.	causing people or things to fall or slide

2. Look at the pictures next to the poem. Read the poem again. Match a picture with one of the people mentioned in the poem. Cirle the words in the poem that helped you.

C. Understanding Similes

1. A simile is a comparison using the words "like" or "as." An example from Sandra Cisneros's story *Hairs* is "My Papa's hair is like a broom." What does a broom look like? Feel like? Read the poem again and answer the questions below.

   a. What is Kiki's hair like? _____

   b. What is Mama's hair like? _____ and

   _____

   c. What does Mama's hair smell like? _____

2. Use your imagination and answer the questions below.

   a. What is "me, my hair" like? _____

   b. What is Carlos's hair like? _____

   c. What is Nenny's hair like? _____

3. How do you think the writer feels about Mama?

4. Use your imagination to complete the sentences below with similes. Share your similes with the class.

   a. The shoes were red like _____

   b. The sun was as hot as _____

   c. The mint ice cream tasted like _____

   d. The wind was as cold as _____

   e. My brother's room smelled like _____

COMMUNICATING YOUR IDEAS

A. Talk About It

Choose a line from the poem that you like the best. Discuss with a partner why you like it.

B. Write About It

Write a description of people in your family or about some friends. Use a few similes.

_____

_____

_____

_____

_____

_____

_____

ONE STEP BEYOND

■ **Internet**

Go to a book shop website, such as amazon.com. Look for Oseola's book, called *Wisdom for Rich Living*. What did customers who read the book say about it? Look for books by Sandra Cisneros. What are the names of some of her other books? What did customers say about *The House on Mango Street*?

■ **More Readings**

Read another Sandra Cisneros story. Find similes.

■ **Music**

Listen to *Wonderful World*. List the academic subjects in the song.

■ **Movies**

Watch *Stand and Deliver*. What did the teacher do to help the students?

■ **Guest Speaker or Campus Visit**

Invite a representative from your school's (or a college near you) counseling or financial aid office to speak to your class about financial assistance and scholarships available for students for college.

■ **Journal**

Write a scholarship letter. Include information about yourself, including your goals and abilities.

■ **Vocabulary**

Copy the words from this unit into your vocabulary log. Use a word web.

■ **CNN®**

Remember to watch the CNN® video clip for this unit.

A BALANCED DIET

GETTING READY

1. Complete the chart with the time expressions below. Then interview a partner.

| several times a day | a few times a week | not very often |
| every day | once a week | never |

How often do you...	Me	My partner
...eat fruit and vegetables?		
...drink coffee?		
...eat bread?		
...eat rice?		
...eat meat?		
...eat dairy products?		
...eat sweets?		

2. Share what you found out with your class.

THE CHOCOLATE MAN

PRE-READING

Look at the photos and the title of the story. What is the article about? Write three things you want to know about the chocolate man?

1. _____

2. _____

3. _____

THE CHOCOLATE MAN

Milton Snavely Hershey was born in 1857 in Pennsylvania. His family was very poor. When Milton was fourteen years old, he started working with a candy maker. Milton liked making candy. Later, he started his own candy business, but the business went bankrupt. He tried again. He opened a candy factory that made caramels. Everyone liked them because they tasted very good. This time, Milton Hershey's business was a success.

   In 1894, Milton Hershey went to the World's Fair. He saw a man from Germany making chocolate bars. Most Americans did not know about chocolate bars, so Milton decided to try making chocolate bars at his caramel factory. Milton and his workers

continued →

created a special recipe for milk chocolate bars. They started selling their new chocolate bars.

It was the first time many Americans tasted milk chocolate. The chocolate bars only cost five cents. They were cheap and delicious, so Hershey's chocolate bars became very popular. Milton's factory started producing many more milk chocolate bars. Milton bought a large dairy in Pennsylvania because his factory needed so much milk to make chocolate. Later, he bought sugar mills in the Caribbean because he needed so much sugar to produce chocolate. In 1907, the company started selling Hershey's Kisses. They were also very popular.

Milton Hershey became very wealthy. He decided to build a special town because he wanted to take care of his factory workers. He built modern houses, a big park, a garden, schools, a baseball field and a zoo. People who lived in the town worked at the chocolate factory. Milton was one of the first factory owners to give his workers benefits. He gave them health insurance. What was the name of this new town? The name of the new town was Hershey, of course! The names of two streets in the new town were Cocoa Avenue and Chocolate Avenue!

Milton and his wife Kitty also built a special school in the town of Hershey. It was a school for orphan boys. The boys went to school, lived and worked on farms and learned skills for their jobs. When Milton Hershey died in 1945, he gave all of his money to the school for orphan children. Today, the school has one thousand students. Hershey, Pennsylvania is still a nice place, so many tourists enjoy visiting it. People call Hershey "The Town that Smells Like Chocolate."

READING AND WORD STUDY SKILLS

A. Understanding the Main Ideas

Circle the correct word to complete each sentence.

1. Milton Hershey made *candy / milk chocolate* popular in the United States.

2. Milton Hershey made a lot of *money / parks*.

3. Milton Hershey built a *special town / museum* for his workers.

4. Hershey built a special *school / toy* for orphan boys.

5. Today, Hershey, Pennsylvania, is a nice place to live, and *cows /tourists* like to visit there for sightseeing.

B. Finding Details

Each sentence has one mistake. Correct the mistakes.

Example: *At first, a Hershey milk chocolate bar cost* ~~fifteen~~ *five cents.*

1. In 1907, Hershey's company started selling caramels.

2. Milton bought a large dairy farm because his factory needed sugar to make chocolate.

3. Milton Hershey was one of the first factory owners to give his workers kisses for working at his company.

4. Milton Hershey died in 1954.

C. Drawing Conclusions

Circle the correct answer. Circle T for true, F for false and ITK for impossible to know.

1. Milton Hershey wanted to take care of his workers.	T	F	ITK
2. Milton and Kitty did not like children.	T	F	ITK
3. Milton and Kitty had a big family.	T	F	ITK
4. Milton Hershey gave a lot of money to the school.	T	F	ITK
5. Hershey's chocolate is the most popular chocolate in the world.	T	F	ITK

D. Learning New Words

Look at the words in the text and choose the correct definition.

1. He opened a candy factory that made caramels. Everyone liked them because they tasted very good. This time, Milton Hershey's business was a **success**.
   Success means

   a. a good event   b. a bad event   c. an easy event

2. He decided to build a special town because he wanted to **take care of** his factory workers.
   Take care of means

       a. buy   b. see   c. provide for

3. They were cheap and delicious, so Hershey's chocolate bars became very **popular**.
   Popular means

       a. expensive   b. well-liked   c. good

E. Learning New Words

Draw a line from the word to its definition.

1. create		a. children with no parents
2. recipe		b. to experience a flavor
3. taste		c. rich
4. delicious		d. to make
5. wealthy		e. new, up-to-date
6. orphans		f. directions for cooking something
7. modern		g. good-tasting

F. Using New Words

Work with a partner. Write five questions using vocabulary words from above. Then ask your classmates the questions.

Example: *What popular singer do you like?*

1. _____

2. _____

3. _____

4. _____

5. _____

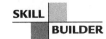
G. Sentence Connectors

1. We use words like **because** and **so** to link or join two ideas together.

Because answers the question "why." **Because** shows reason.
Example: *I like chocolate because it's delicious*

So answers the question "what happened." **So** shows result.
Example: *I ate too much chocolate, so I got sick.*

Look back at the story. Finish the sentences correctly in the box.

1. Everyone liked them	because	
2. Most Americans did not know about chocolate bars	so	
3. They were cheap and delicious	so	
4. Milton bought a large dairy in Pennsylvania	because	
5. Hershey, Pennsylvania is still a nice place	so	

2. Write four sentences about yourself using "so" and "because."

1. _____

2. _____

3. _____

4. _____

COMMUNICATING YOUR IDEAS

Talk About It

You need a marker for each player and one die.

Directions: Put your marker on START. Each person in your group rolls the die. The person with the highest number goes first. The first player rolls again and moves his marker the number of spaces indicated on the die. As each player lands on a square, she answers the question or follows the directions on the square. Play continues clockwise. The first player to reach the FINISH space wins the game.

1. **START**	2. What are your favorite candy bars?	3. It's your lucky day! **MOVE AHEAD 2 SPACES.**	4. What are the two main ingredients of chocolate?
8. If you had a town of your own, what would it smell like?	7. You ate too much chocolate! **LOSE A TURN!**	6. Describe your favorite chocolate dessert.	5. Do you think Milton Hershey was a good boss? Explain.
9. Would you like to visit the town of Hershey? Explain.	10. You are very sweet! **ROLL THE DIE AGAIN!**	11. How often do you eat something made with chocolate?	12. What animals do you think you can find at the Hershey Zoo?
16. **FINISH**	15. Would you like to work in a chocolate factory? Explain.	14. **LOSE A TURN!** You have seven cavities from eating too much candy.	13. What do you know about chocolate?

YOUR GUIDE TO HEALTHY EATING

PRE-READING

What are your favorite foods? Look at the pictures and the column labeled "Food." Circle the ones you like best. Discuss with your group which foods you like best and why. Read the poster. How can food help you be healthy?

Your Guide to Healthy Eating

Your body needs lots of nutrients so it can be healthy. Eating different foods will help your body get all of the nutrients it needs. Look at the table below to learn what you can eat to be healthy.

Food	Nutrients	Benefit
carrots, broccoli, cantaloupe	Vitamin A	helps make healthy eyes
whole wheat, brown rice, beans	Vitamin B-1	helps turn food into energy
oranges, kiwis, tomatoes	Vitamin C	helps the body fight disease
tofu, beef	iron	helps carry oxygen in blood
yogurt, milk, cheese	calcium	helps make healthy bones and teeth
fish, chicken	protein	helps the body build muscles

Remember:
· DON'T eat too many fatty foods such as ice-cream and fries.
· DON'T eat too many sweet foods such as soda, dessert and candy.
· DON'T eat too many salty foods such as chips and pizza.
· DO eat lots of foods with fiber such as whole wheat bread, fruit and vegetables.
· DO drink 8 glasses of water every day.

Glossary:
benefit – gain, positive result
nutrient – any of the substances contained in food that are essential to life
energy – the power to do work or be active

READING AND WORD STUDY SKILLS

A. Understanding the Main Ideas

Check (✓) the sentences that are true based on the reading.

1. _____ You should never eat pizza.

2. _____ Eating a variety of foods is a good idea.

3. _____ Drink a lot of milk.

4. _____ Eat a lot of fruit and vegetables.

5. _____ Many foods have good things in them that our bodies need.

B. Finding Details

1. Draw a line from the food to its nutrient or benefit.

   a. beef   vitamin C

   b. tomatoes   helps carry oxygen in blood

   c. carrots   helps make healthy eyes

   d. fish   vitamin B-1

   e. whole wheat   protein

   f. milk   helps make healthy bones and teeth

2. Circle T for true and F for false. Discuss in pairs why you chose your answers.

   a. It is a good idea to drink lots of soda.   T   F

   b. It is a good idea to eat lots of chocolate.   T   F

   c. It is a good idea to eat lots of fries.   T   F

   d. It is a good idea to eat carrots.   T   F

C. Learning New Words

Write the word next to the correct definition

healthy	muscle	sweet	salty	fatty	disease

1. _____ body tissues on the bones that make the body move

2. _____ containing a lot of fat

3. _____ having the taste of salt

4. _____ a sickness or serious disorder that is caused by infection or bad living conditions

5. _____ having a taste like sugar or honey

6. _____ in good health

D. Using New Words

Circle the correct word.

1. Donuts taste very _salty/sweet_.

2. I shouldn't eat too much _healthy/fatty_ food like fries and burgers.

3. Kazuko is very _healthy/disease_. She eats lots of fruits and vegetables.

4. Pablo likes _salty/sweet_ foods such as peanuts and chips.

5. Malaria is a type of _sweet/disease_.

E. Word Partnerships

Some words are often grouped or used together. For example "bread and butter" "strong wind" "next year." Knowing that some words are often in groups can help you read faster.

Look at the words in the box. Do you know what they mean? Use your dictionary to help. Match the words to the picture.

fast food	junk food	fresh food	frozen food

Draw a line to connect the word partners.

a. TV	potato
b. couch	meal
c. fresh	dinner
d. four-course	fruit
e. second	serving

COMMUNICATING YOUR IDEAS

A. Talk About It

Discuss the questions with a small group.

1. Do you eat healthy food?

2. What foods from the lists above are your favorites? How do you prepare them?

3. What foods do you think you should eat more of? What foods do you think you should eat less of?

4. Are the foods you usually eat in the U.S. similar or different from what you usually eat in your native country?

5. What are the basic foods in your native country?

6. Do you like junk food or fresh food?

7. Describe a popular dish in your family.

B. Write About It

Write a description of a food. Read your description to your group or class. Your classmates will guess what food you described.

Example: *What food is it? It is brown on the outside. It is orange on the inside. It is hard. To eat it, you have to cook it. It is sweet. It has vitamin A in it. It can make healthy eyes. (It's a sweet potato!)*

MY TRUE LOVE

PRE-READING

Julie Diaz has written an article for her college newspaper about chocolate. Read the last paragraphs of the article. What does Julie think about chocolate?

1. Julie thinks chocolate is bad for you

2. Julie thinks chocolate is good for you

3. Julie thinks eating a little chocolate is okay

POINT OF VIEW	FEBRUARY 13

My True Love
By Julie Diaz

Last week, I saw a doctor on TV saying, "Don't give chocolates on Valentine's Day." He said that chocolate is unhealthy. However, other people say chocolate helps them feel better when they are miserable. What's the truth? I searched on the Internet for interesting facts about chocolate.

Chocolate is made using beans from the cacao tree. The cacao tree is from Central and South America. Christopher Columbus was the first European to see cacao in 1502. In some parts of Central and South America, cacao beans were used like money. When Spanish conquistador Hernando Cortez brought cacao beans back to Spain  in about 1522, the beans were like treasure.

Believe it or not, chocolate can be healthy. Some types of chocolate, especially dark chocolate, have important nutrients called minerals that we need. In addition, many people feel good after they eat chocolate. Chocolate contains stimulants, which are chemicals that often make us feel happy. Scientists want to find out more about how chocolate makes us feel.

However, doctors say that eating too much chocolate may cause health problems. Chocolate is a fatty food. It contains a lot of saturated fats. Too many saturated fats can lead to heart disease and obesity.

After my search on the Internet, I feel happy to continue eating a little chocolate. And I hope my sweetie will be sweet to me by giving me my favorite sweet on Valentine's Day!

READING AND WORD STUDY SKILLS

A. Understanding the Main Ideas

There are five paragraphs in the article. Each paragraph has one main idea. This idea gives you the most important information the writer wants to communicate. Which paragraph contains the following main ideas?

1. Benefits of chocolate   Paragraph: _____

2. History of chocolate   Paragraph: _____

3. Julie's conclusion   Paragraph: _____

4. Bad things about chocolate   Paragraph: _____

5. Introduction   Paragraph: *1*

B. Finding Details

Complete the sentences from the reading. Sometimes more than one word is needed.

Paragraph 1	He said that chocolate is _____. Other people say chocolate _____ better.
Paragraph 2	Chocolate is made using _____ from the cocoa tree. The cacao tree is from _____. _____ was the first European to see cacao in 1502. Cacao beans were used like _____.
Paragraph 3	Some types of chocolate contain important _____. In addition, many people feel _____.
Paragraph 4	However, doctors say that eating too much chocolate may cause _____. Chocolate is a _____.
Paragraph 5	After my search I feel _____ to continue eating chocolate.

C. Learning New Words

Circle the word(s) that mean the same as the word(s) in bold.

1. I **searched** on the Internet for interesting facts about chocolate.
   Searched means

   a. looked for something   b. helped someone   c. moved something

2. Other people say chocolate helps them feel better when they are miserable.
   Miserable means

   a. happy   b. silly   c. sad

3. Scientists want to **find out** more about how chocolate makes us feel.
   Find out means

   a. eat   b. learn   c. hear

D. Using New Words

Write a sentence using each of the words above

1. _____

2. _____

3. _____

COMMUNICATING YOUR IDEAS

A. Write About It

Go on the Internet or go to the library and find information about coffee, sugar, peanuts, or some other food product. Use the chart below to make notes. Present your information to the class.

Main Ideas	Details
1. Introduction	
2. History	
3. Benefits	
4. Bad things	
5. Your thoughts	

B. Write About It

Write about a favorite food from your native country. Include the nutrients contained in the food. Include what the food tastes like. Share it with your class.

Example: *Brownies are a popular chocolate dessert in the United States. People like to eat them at picnics, barbecues and at home. Brownies are made of chocolate. They are not very healthy and do not have many nutrients. But they taste sweet and delicious!*

■ **Internet**

Visit the Hershey, Pennsylvania website www.hersheys.com. Find out how chocolate is made.

■ **More Readings**

Read articles from the food section of your local newspaper or a cooking magazine. Explain to your classmates how to prepare a food you read about.

■ **Movies and Music**

Willie Wonka and the Chocolate Factory is a book and a movie. Read the book or watch the movie. Then write a summary of the story in your journal. Practice listening with *The Candyman,* a song from the movie. Find the rhymes in the song.

■ **Guest Speaker**

Invite a nutritionist or nurse to your class to give a presentation about nutrition. Prepare questions to ask beforehand and take notes as you listen.

■ **Food Pyramid Guide**

Look on the Internet for the food pyramid guide. What are the food groups in the pyramid? How many servings should we eat from each group every day?

■ **Blind Chocolate Taste Test**

Bring different kinds of chocolate into your classroom. Taste the chocolate and vote on which one is the best!

■ **Vocabulary**

Copy the words from this unit into your vocabulary log. Use Word Webs. Use Word Partnerships.

■ **CNN.**

Remember to watch the CNN® video clip for this unit.

HEROES

GETTING READY

1. Work with a partner. Who are the people in the photos? What do they do?
   Do you think the people in the photos are heroes? Why or why not?

2. What qualities make a hero? Circle the adjectives below that you think
   describe a hero.

beautiful	wise	strong	handsome
intelligent	generous	tall	caring
happy	brave	rich	friendly

4. Do you think Oseola McCarty from Unit 4 and Milton Hershey from Unit 5
   were heroes? Explain. Which qualities from the list above did they have?

INTERNET HEROES

PRE-READING

1. The words below are from the story. Write N for noun, V for verb, or A for adjective.

   Sean _N_   girl____   typed____   Internet____   dizzy____

   sick____   message____   called____   paramedics____

2. Look at the words above and the pictures below. Discuss in pairs what you think happens in the story. Write your predictions and share them with your class.

INTERNET HEROES

Taija was alone one night, working on a computer in a university library. She was doing research on the Internet. Suddenly she felt ill. She was dizzy and hot. She had a lot of pain. She couldn't move her legs, and she couldn't get to the telephone to call for help. No one was in the library to help her. What could she do? Who would help?

Meanwhile, in Texas, Sean came home from school and sat down at his computer. He got on the Internet and entered his favorite chat room, a place where people from all over the world can have a conversation on the computer at the same time. As Sean was reading the conversations in the chat room, he saw an unusual message: "WOULD SOMEONE HELP ME?"

Sean was surprised. At first, he thought it was a joke. Capital letters in chat rooms and email usually mean someone is shouting. Sean knew that he couldn't believe everything he read on the Internet, but then he saw another strange message: "I CAN'T BREATHE. HELP ME!" Sean was worried. The other people in the chat room were not paying attention to her. "Is she playing a joke?" Sean asked himself. He typed, "Is this a game? Can you call 911?"

Sean asked more questions. Soon he learned that it was true! A girl named Taija was sick and needed help. "Where are you?" he asked. The girl answered, "Finland." Sean was shocked because Texas is so far from Finland!

Sean called to his mother. He told his mom about Taija. Sean and his mother wanted to help the girl, so they called the sheriff's department in Texas. Sean gave the sheriff's department Taija's telephone and address in Finland. Next, the sheriff's department called an international operator. Then the international operator called emergency services in Finland. The operator gave them Taija's address. Sean and his mother stayed on the computer for almost two hours with Taija, waiting for help to arrive.

Finally, paramedics arrived to help Taija. They looked for her in the library. The library was now closed and dark. She could hear the paramedics running in the halls. They were looking for her, but she was too weak to call out to them. At last, they found her.

Later, the sheriff's department in Texas received a message about Taija. She was at the hospital, and she was okay. She wanted to thank Sean for helping her. Sean smiled when he heard the news. He felt like a hero.

READING AND WORD STUDY SKILLS

A. Understanding the Main Ideas

Circle the correct answer.

1. Sean read a strange computer message. He was

   a. worried.   b. not interested.   c. amazed.

2. Sean and Taija communicated

   a. by talking on the   b. on the computer.   c. by shouting.
      telephone.

3. Taija had a problem. She was

   a. hungry.   b. lonely.   c. sick.

4. To get help, Taija

   a. typed a message   b. called her mother   c. called an
      on the Internet.   on the telephone.   ambulance.

B. Finding Details

Draw a line to complete the sentences from the reading.

1. Sean knew that he couldn't   a. because Texas is far from
   believe everything he read on   Finland.
   the Internet,

2. Sean was shocked   b. because they wanted to wait
                                           for help.

3. Sean and his mother stayed   c. but she was too weak to call
   on the computer for almost   to them.
   two hours with Taija

4. The paramedics were looking   d. but then he saw another
   for her,   strange message.

C. Drawing Conclusions

Circle T for true, F for false or ITK for Impossible to Know.

1. Taija is a student.   T   F   ITK

2. Sean and his mother are concerned
   about other people.   T   F   ITK

3. Everyone in Finland has a computer.   T   F   ITK

4. Sean doesn't think everything he reads
on the Internet is true.   T   F   ITK

5. Taija speaks more than one language.   T   F   ITK

6. Sean wants to be a computer
programmer in the future.   T   F   ITK

D. Using New Words

Complete the sentances with the correct words.

trouble	dizzy	paramedics	entered	strange

1. Yesterday I was sick. I had a headache and felt _____.

2. The movie star _____ the room and everyone clapped.

3. _____ and firefighters work together to help people
who have accidents.

4. Last night, we heard a _____ noise in our backyard.

5. My friend had _____ finding a job because she doesn't
speak English.

message	pay attention	pain	weak	alone

6. The teacher said, "Students, please _____."

7. Stefan called the manager on the telephone. She wasn't there, so he
left a _____ for her.

8. A toothache is _____ in a tooth.

9. I like being with people. I don't like being _____.

10. Elena is not very strong. She is _____.

E. Synonyms

In Unit 3, you learned about antonyms. Antonyms are opposite words. Synonyms are words that have similar meanings. *Small* and *little* are synonyms. *Big* and *large* are synonyms. Learning synonyms can help you remember and improve your vocabulary. Underline the synonyms in the sentences from "Internet Heroes." The first one has been done for you.

1. Taija was <u>sick</u> and needed help.
   She felt <u>ill</u>.

2. Sean saw an unusual message.
   He saw another strange message.

3. The paramedics searched for Taija in the library.
   They were looking for her.

4. Finally, paramedics arrived to help Taija.
   At last, they found her.

COMMUNICATING YOUR IDEAS

A. Talk About It

Discuss the following questions with a small group. Then report back to the class.

1. What do you use computers for at work? At home? At school?

2. Do you use the Internet? What do you use it for?

3. Would you like to learn to use computers more? What would you like to learn? How can you learn more?

B. Doing a Survey

1. Take a poll of your class. In the chart below, write the number of students who use the computer in the seven ways listed.

ACTIVITY	1. type papers on the computer	2. use email	3. use chat rooms	4. research infor- mation on the Internet	5. use a computer at work	6. download music or videos from the Internet	7. play computer games
NUMBER OF STUDENTS							

2. Now work with your teacher in class to make a bar graph with the information from your class poll.

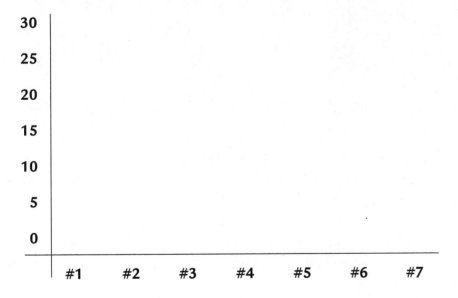

3. Write a summary of what you found out in your survey.

MOTHER TERESA

PRE-READING

1. Do you know who the people are in the photos? Why are they famous? Discuss in pairs.

2. Have you heard of the Nobel Peace Prize? It's an international prize given to people who make outstanding contributions to world peace. The people in the photos above won the Nobel Peace Prize. Do you know why they won it?

3. You're going to read a short biography of Mother Teresa taken from an encyclopedia. Quickly scan the biography. Why are the following numbers important?

    a. 1910
    b. 1997

MOTHER TERESA

(1910-1997) Mother Teresa was born in 1910 in Skopje, Albania. Her real name was Agnes Gonxha Bojaxhiu. She was from a devout Catholic family who helped poor people in their neighborhood. She studied languages and read books about missionaries. When Mother Teresa was 12, she decided to give her life to service for God. When she was 18, she went to Ireland to become a Catholic sister. A year later, she went to India. She chose the name Teresa from Saint Teresa of Lisieux, the patron saint of foreign missionaries. First, she was a principal at a Roman Catholic high school in Calcutta, India. But she saw many sick and dying poor people in the streets of India. Mother Teresa was very concerned, so in 1948, she began working with poor people. She brought them medicine, clothes and food. She taught the children to read and write. In 1950, Mother Teresa and her sisters started the Missionaries of Charity, a group of women who work with the very poor and dying. They made many sacrifices to help the poor. In 1952, Mother Teresa opened the Pure Heart Home for poor dying people in Calcutta. Eventually, Mother Teresa and her Missionaries of Charity worked all over the world to help poor people. She opened homes and schools for them. Mother Teresa received the Nobel Peace Prize in 1979. *Mother Teresa: In My Own Words*, a collection of her ideas and thoughts, was published in 1996. She died in 1997.

READING AND WORD STUDY SKILLS

A. Understanding the Main Ideas

Write three things Mother Teresa did to help people.

1. _____

2. _____

3. _____

B. Making a Timeline

SKILL BUILDER

1. Making a timeline is a good way to organize information. A timeline can help you understand all the facts in a reading. It can also help you prepare to write. Scan the reading about Mother Teresa. Find the information you need to complete the timeline.

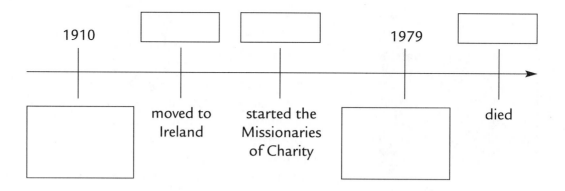

1910   [ ]   [ ]   1979   [ ]

[ ]   moved to Ireland   started the Missionaries of Charity   [ ]   died

C. Using a Dictionary

1. Read the sentences below from *Mother Teresa* again. Can you guess what the word in bold means?

    a. Mother Teresa was very **concerned**, so in 1948, she began working with poor people.

    b. They made many **sacrifices** to help the poor.

    c. She was from a **devout** Catholic family who helped poor people in their neighborhood.

    d. First, she was a **principal** at a Roman Catholic high school in Calcutta, India.

2. Read the definitions below from the *Newbury House Dictionary of American English*. Write the words in bold from above next to the correct definition.

---

sacrifice *noun* **1** loss, or giving up something valuable for a specific purpose.

_____ *verb* **2** to deal with, care about, or worry about.

_____ *noun* **1** the head of a school.

_____ *adjective* **1** deeply religious.

COMMUNICATING YOUR IDEAS

A. Talk About It

Discuss these questions with your group.

1. What heroes did you have when you were a child?

2. Who are some people you admire? Why do you admire them?

3. Are heroes always famous? Are heroes always wealthy?

4. Are famous people always heroes? Can you think of famous people that you do not admire?

5. As a group, make a list of people you admire. Then put your list on the board in your classroom. Compare lists with the other groups. Are there some names that are the same?

B. Interviewing

1. Talk to three people at your school or in your community. Ask them the questions below and take notes in the chart.

2. In class, write the names of the heroes from your interviews on the board. Compare the names to the list your class wrote in the previous section. Are there some names that are similar?

What is your name?	Who is your hero?	Why do you think this person is a hero?

3. Write about what you found out during your interviews.

THE LION AND THE MOUSE

PRE-READING

A fable is a short story or poem. A fable has a special lesson. This lesson shows a moral truth. Fables usually have animals that talk and act like people. Look at the picture and title. What do you think happens in the fable?

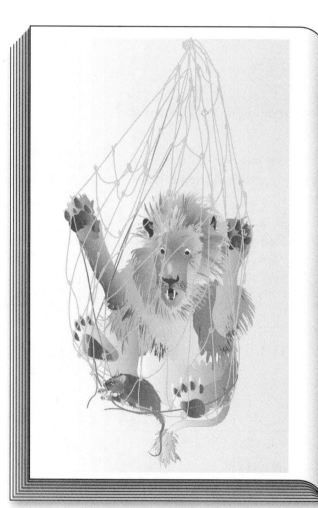

THE LION AND THE MOUSE

One day, a Lion was sleeping in the forest. A shy Mouse accidentally came upon the Lion. When she saw the Lion, the Mouse was so scared, she ran right across the Lion's nose. The Lion woke up suddenly. Angrily, he put his huge paw on the Mouse. The poor Mouse begged, "Please let me go. Don't kill me and some day I will repay your kindness!" The Lion laughed. How could a Mouse ever help a Lion? But he let the Mouse go.

Some days later, the Lion got caught in a hunter's net. His angry roars filled the forest. The Mouse heard the Lion. She ran to the Lion and bit through the net with her teeth. In this way, the Mouse set the Lion free. "Now you know: even a tiny Mouse can help a Lion," she said.

READING AND WORD STUDY SKILLS

A. Understanding the Main Ideas

Put the sentences in the right order.

1. _____ The Lion laughed and let the Mouse go.

2. _____ The Mouse helped the Lion.

3. _____ The Mouse said, "Let me go! I will repay you"

4. _____ The Lion got caught in a hunter's net.

5. __1__ A Lion was sleeping in the forest.

6. _____ The Lion caught a Mouse.

B. Summarizing

SKILL BUILDER

A summary is a short paragraph that gives only the most important information of a story. Write a short summary of the story above. Use the sentences from exercise A.

The Lion and the Mouse

_____

_____

_____

_____

C. Finding Details

Circle the correct answer.

1. The Mouse felt _____ when she saw the Lion.

   a. happy   b. frightened   c. sad

2. The Lion put his _____ on the Mouse.

   a. nose   b. mouth   c. foot

3. The Lion_____ when the Mouse said that she would help the Lion some day.

   a. laughed   b. roared   c. ate the Mouse

4. The Mouse used her _____ to help the Lion.

   a. feet   b. friends   c. teeth

D. Learning New Words

Unscramble the words. Then draw a line from the word to its definition.

1. ent _____   a. a loud, scary sound

2. aorr _____   b. past tense of to catch

3. thagcu _____   c. doing something with anger

4. lygrani _____   d. a material made of string knotted or twisted together

E. Using New Words

Write sentences using the words above.

1. _____

2. _____

3. _____

4. _____

G. Adverbs

SKILL BUILDER

An adverb describes a verb in a sentence. Adverbs give us more information about an action. Adverbs answer the question "How?" See the Appendix on page xx for more information.

Example: *A shy Mouse **accidentally** came upon the Lion.*

1. Complete the chart with adverbs.

Adjective	Adverb
happy	happily
loud	
beautiful	
near	
usual	

2. Complete the sentences with either an adjective or adverb.

   a. Martin _____ hit his drum. It made quite a noise.

   b. My baby Brian laughs _____.

   c. For breakfast I _____ have cereal.

   d. What a nice picture! You paint _____.

   e. I wasn't looking where I was going. I _____ had an accident.

COMMUNICATING YOUR IDEAS

A. Talk About It

Talk with a small group about the questions.

   1. There are many fables like "The Lion and the Mouse." Do you know other fables? Tell one to your group.

   2. Do you know other stories about everyday heroes?

   3. Have you had an everyday hero in your life? Explain.

   4. Are you someone's hero? When have you been a hero? Explain.

B. Write About It

Write your answers to the questions below. Then discuss your answers in pairs.

   1. Do the animals think and act like people in "The Lion and the Mouse"?

   If yes, how? _____

   2. What is the moral of this fable? _____

   _____

   3. Is the Mouse a hero? Why?_____

   _____

   4. Look back to the first page of this unit (p 81). What words from the

   list of qualities describe the Mouse? _____

   _____

■ **Internet Assignment and Presentation**

Find a partner. Go to the library or use the Internet to find information about one of your heroes. Write the answers to the questions below. Then share the information with your class.

Where and when was this person born?
If dead, when did this person die?
What made this person famous?
What are some important or interesting facts you learned about this person?
Do you think this famous person is a hero? Why or why not?

■ **More Readings**

The newspaper often has stories about everyday heroes. Look in your local newspaper this week for stories about everyday heroes. Bring the article to share with your class.

■ **Music**

Listen to a popular song like Mariah Carey's "Hero." Who is the hero in this song? Or listen to Bette Midler's "Wind Beneath My Wings." What did her hero do for her?

■ **Movies**

There are many movies about heroes. Some examples are Rocky and The Motorcycle Diaries. Watch a movie about a hero and write a very short summary about the story. Then use the words you used in this unit to describe the hero.

■ **Journal**

Are you a hero? What hero qualities do you have? Write about yourself in your journal.

■ **Vocabulary**

Copy the words from this unit into your vocabulary log.

■ **CNN.**

Remember to watch the CNN® video clip for this unit.

OCEAN LIFE

GETTING READY

How much do you know about ocean life? Work with a group to do the Ocean Quiz.

The Ocean Quiz

Complete each sentence with a number from the box

36,000	2	75	25
6	77	40	5

1. Oceans cover _____% of the earth's surface.

2. There are about _____ oceans in the world.

3. The deepest part of the ocean is _____ feet below sea level.

4. Penguins can swim up to _____ miles per hour.

5. Some whales can hold their breath for up to _____ hours.

6. Crabs have _____ walking legs.

7. _____ million tourists visit the beaches in Hawaii each year.

8. _____% of U.S. waters are too polluted for swimming or fishing.

SHARK ATTACK!

PRE-READING

1. Look at the title and picture. What's happening? What's about to happen?

2. The paragraphs below are from the story about Joe. Read the paragraphs and put them into the correct order.

Without warning, a shark burst out the water.	

Finally, he was safe.	

Somehow, Joe swam to the beach.	

Joe walked from his house to the beach.	*1*

He got his body board and went into the water.	

The shark was attacking the body board	

SHARK ATTACK!

Joe loved the ocean. He loved surfing and sail boarding. His job was making surfboards and body boards. He also taught people how to sail board. He said, "The ocean is my playground."

One day, Joe walked from his house on the island of Kauai to his favorite beach. The sky and the ocean were a beautiful blue. He put on his fins, got his body board and went into the water. He paddled quickly past the waves. He was startled when he saw a dark shape in the water. Then he relaxed. It was a large sea turtle. Joe lay on his body board. He was waiting for a wave.

Suddenly, without warning, a shark burst out of the water. Joe was eye to eye with a tiger shark. The shark had the nose of the body board and Joe's arms in its mouth. The shark pulled Joe and his body board under the water. Joe pulled his left

continued →

hand out of the shark's mouth. He tried to hit the shark on the nose. Then the shark pulled at the body board and turned away. Joe fell off the body board.

Joe lay on his back in the water and kicked his feet fast. He wanted to escape. He watched the shark. It was attacking the body board. Then Joe looked at his right arm. His hand and wrist were gone. His arm was bleeding badly and the blood made a red trail in the water. Joe didn't panic. He put pressure on his arm to stop the bleeding. He knew the shark might smell the blood. Joe kicked and kicked. He held his arm and yelled, "Help! Help!" The shark was still with the bodyboard. When Joe reached the beach, he ran for help. A tourist came to help him, and paramedics took Joe to the hospital. Joe was safe.

Today Joe's life is very different from before the shark attack. He doesn't make surfboards or teach sail boarding any more. He works at a college with students with disabilities. He patiently helps them because he knows how hard they have to work. Joe had to rehabilitate his arms and hands. He gradually learned to use them well again. Now he has an artificial right hand and arm.

"Sometimes it is hard," says Joe, "but I have learned how to be grateful. My experience taught me a lot about patience for myself and for others."

READING AND WORD STUDY SKILLS

A. Understanding the Main Ideas

1. Circle other possible titles for the story.

    a. Eye to Eye with a Shark
    b. Students with Disabilities
    c. A Helpful Tourist
    d. Blood in the Water
    e. Dangerous Sports

2. Circle the word(s) to complete each sentence correctly.

    a. Joe liked the <u>ocean/sharks</u>.

    b. One day, Joe went <u>bodyboarding/fishing</u>.

    c. A shark bit Joe's <u>arms/legs</u>.

    d. Joe swam to the <u>beach/boat</u>.

    e. Today, Joe has an artificial <u>leg/arm</u>.

    f. Today, Joe works at a college with students <u>with disabilities/studying English</u>.

B. Finding Details

Write the correct letter to complete each sentence.

1. _____ Before the shark attack, Joe   a. a red trail in the water.

2. _____ Suddenly, Joe was eye to eye with   b. works at a college.

3. _____ The person who helped Joe on the beach was   c. a tourist.

4. _____ Blood from Joe's arm made   d. taught water sports.

5. _____ Joe put pressure on   e. his arm.

6. _____ Today, Joe   f. a shark.

C. Learning New Words

grateful	escaped	artificial	kicked	might

Complete the sentences with the words from the list above.

1. The baby _____ her feet and smiled because she was happy.

2. My mom looks after the kids when I work. I'm very _____ for her help.

3. My brother lost his leg in a car crash. Now he has an _____ leg.

4. The police were chasing the robber, but the robber _____.

5. If I have time, I _____ go shopping later.

| patience | fell off | gradually | quickly | disability |

1. A mom and dad need lots of _____ when they have a new baby.

2. It's taking a long time, but _____ I'm learning to speak English.

3. When I was learning to ride a bike, I _____ all the time.

4. My friend has a _____. He can't hear.

5. I was late for work, so I ran _____.

D. Grouping Words

1. A good way to remember new words is to put them into groups. A common way to group words is by part of speech (noun, verb, adjective, etc). Putting words into groups can help you see how words are related to each other. See page 129 for more information.

2. Put the words from the box into the correct columns.

| grateful | escaped | artificial | kicked | might |
| patience | fell off | gradually | quickly | disability |

Noun	Verb	Adjective	Adverb
1.	1.	1.	1.
2.	2.	2.	2.
	3.		
	4.		

3. Write four sentences using the words from the chart.

a. _____

b. _____

c. _____

d. _____

E. Before or After?

Put a check (✔) in the correct column to describe Joe's life before and after the shark attack.

	Before the attack	After the attack
1. Joe works at a college with disabled students.		
2. Joe lived in Kauai.		
3. He knows how disabled students feel from his personal experience.		
4. He uses an artificial arm.		
5. He taught water sports.		
6. He learned to be grateful.		

F. Drawing Conclusions

Circle the correct answer.

1. When Joe saw something in the water, he thought it was _____

    a. another surfer.   b. a turtle.

2. Joe was afraid that the shark might smell the blood because _____

    a. sharks are attracted to blood.   b. sharks are scared of blood.

3. Joe knows how students with disabilities feel because _____

    a. his landlord is disabled.   b. he is disabled, too.

COMMUNICATING YOUR IDEAS

A. Talk About It

Talk about the following questions with your group.

1. Do you like water sports such as surfing, boating, fishing and scuba diving? Why or why not? Is there a water sport you would like to learn?

2. Where is Hawaii? Find it on the map of the U.S. Have you ever visited Hawaii? Would you like to visit Hawaii?

3. Do you know a person with a disability? Describe his or her disability to your group.

4. What are some different kinds of disabilities?

5. What kind of assistance for people with disabilities is available in your town?

B. Roleplaying

1. If you could interview Joe, what questions would you ask? Write two or three questions you would like to ask Joe.

   1. _____

   2. _____

   3. _____

2. Work with a partner. One student is Joe, the other is the interviewer.

PART TWO · SHARKS: SAFER THAN SODA MACHINES

PRE-READING

1. What do you know about sharks? Write T for true or F for false.

   a. _____ All sharks attack people.

   b. _____ The movie *Jaws* is based on a true story.

   c. _____ There are about 400 kinds of sharks.

   d. _____ Sometimes people find sharks in lakes and rivers.

   e. _____ Sharks have no bones.

   f. _____ Sharks have 34 teeth, just like people.

2. Read the article to see if you are right.

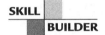

READING AND WORD STUDY SKILLS

A. Using Titles to Understand the Main Ideas

Some articles have subtitles, titles within the reading before a paragraph. Reading the title and subtitles before the rest of the article can help you understand quickly what the main ideas are. Only look at the title and subtitles. Then decide if the statements are true or false.

1. Everyone thinks sharks are scary.   T   F

2. Sharks are boring animals.   T   F

3. Some sharks can kill people.   T   F

4. Sharks are safe from people.   T   F

5. Sharks help the world.   T   F

B. Finding Details

Find the information you need to complete the chart on page 105.

SHARKS
SAFER THAN SODA MACHINES!

40% Are Scared of Sharks

Are you scared of sharks? A recent survey found nearly 40% of people are scared of sharks. Some people blame movies like *Jaws*. In reality, sharks are more scared of people. In fact, sharks are safer than soda machines!

Sharks Are Amazing Animals

There are almost 400 kinds of sharks. Some sharks live in rivers. Their eyesight is excellent. In fact, they see ten times better than people. They have no bones, just cartilage. Your ears are made of cartilage. Every couple of weeks, most sharks lose their teeth and produce new teeth. They can have up to 50,000 teeth in a lifetime. Their sense of smell is amazing. For example, they can smell blood from two miles away.

Most Sharks Are Not Dangerous

Most people think that all sharks are dangerous, but this is not true. Most sharks eat fish. Only 32 kinds of sharks attack people. There are about 100 shark attacks reported a year, according to shark researchers. Researchers also say that soda machines kill more people than sharks do. The soda machines fall on people when they get angry and kick machines to get a soda or money back.

100 Million Sharks Killed Every Year

In fact, people are more dangerous to sharks than sharks are to people. 100 million sharks are killed each year. People eat shark fin soup and make medicine from shark cartilage. Teeth are used for ornaments. Some sharks are killed for sport.

With Sharks, the World Is a Better Place

We should stop killing sharks. They are part of the important marine food chain. Sharks benefit people too, such as people who work in the fishing industry. Important medical research on sharks may help scientists learn more about how to fight diseases in humans. Are you still scared of sharks?

Topic	Number
1.	40%
2. kinds of sharks	
3.	10 times better than people
4. teeth in a lifetime	
5. can smell blood	
6. kinds of sharks dangerous to people	
7. shark attacks per year	
8.	100 million

C. Understanding New Vocabulary

Unscramble the words from the article. Then draw a line from the word to the correct definition.

recent	ornaments	industry	dangerous

1. noranmntse _____   a. not safe

2. trenec _____   b. a type of trade or manufacturing

3. gerdounas _____   c. in the past but not very long ago

4. dustirny _____   d. things that are decorative rather than useful

D. Using New Vocabulary

Read the sentences below. Circle the right word.

1. Some snakes are very recent/dangerous. They can bite you.

2. The car industry/ornaments makes a lot of money.

3. My grandmother has many recent/ornaments in her house.

4. In dangerous/recent months, there has been a lot of rain.

COMMUNICATING YOUR IDEAS

A. Talk About It

Work with a partner. Which animals are you scared of? Answer the questions below and report back to your class.

1. Is there an animal you are scared of?

2. Is this animal really dangerous for people? Explain.

3. Is this animal endangered? How do people threaten this animal? Explain.

B. Write About It

Write a paragraph about an accident or scary experience you had.

Example:

A Dangerous Swim

Ten years ago, I was on a safari vacation in Senegal, West Africa. It was a hot day. Our group was hiking for many hours through little villages. We came back to our camp, and three of us went swimming in the river. We wanted to swim across the river because we saw hippos in the water. We wanted to get close to them. The hippos were coming toward us. Some people on shore were yelling at us. We were smiling because our friends were taking photos of us. But some people were yelling, "Come out of the water! Quick!" So we swam back and got out of the water. Then we saw the hippos again. They were chasing us. They were protecting their babies. We were in serious danger, but we didn't know it!

PRE-READING

1. Have you ever been to a beach? Was it dirty? What kind of trash did you see?

2. Look at the flyer below. Where do you think you would see this kind of flyer? Would you help clean the beach?

SURF BEACH CLEAN UP DAY
Surf Beach
Saturday, October 12, noon

Please join us for the yearly Surf Beach Clean Up Day. Show that you care. All ages are welcome.

Why do we need your help? Just look at what we collected last year:

3,377 cigarette butts

32 syringes

2,047 food wrappers

10 car tires

1,126 glass bottles

3 mattresses

832 aluminum cans

1 refrigerator

This trash is pollution. It harms people and wildlife. It also makes our beaches unsafe and ugly. So please join us at noon and help clean up the mess.

We can make a difference!

For more information email CleanSurfBeach@coolmail.net.

READING AND WORD STUDY SKILLS

A. Understanding the Main Ideas

Circle the correct answer

1. This is a flyer that _____.

    a. is asking people for money   b. is asking people for help

2. Volunteers are needed to _____.

    a. clean up the beach   b. plan a meeting

3. There is _____ of trash at Surf Beach.

    a. a lot   b. a little

4. Trash on the beach _____ wildlife, people and the water.

    a. helps   b. hurts

B. Finding Details

1. Look back at the reading and draw a line to match the number with the trash item.

    a. 32   mattresses

    b. 3,377   cigarette butts

    c. 832   car tires

    d. 10   aluminum cans

    e. 3   syringes

2. Answer the questions below:

    a. When is the beach clean up? _____

    b. Who can go? _____

    c. How can you find out more? _____

C. Learning New Words

Read the sentences below. Guess the meaning of the word(s) in bold. Do not use your dictionary. Circle the correct definition.

1. All ages are **welcome**.
   Welcome means
   a. accepted happily or gratefully
   b. not wanted
   c. needed very soon

2. This trash can seriously **harm** our seabirds and marine life.
   Harm means
   a. burn
   b. hurt
   c. cut

3. So, please join in and help **clean up** the **mess**.
   Clean up means
   a. to make a place dirty
   b. to make a place happy
   c. to make a place cleaner

   Mess means
   d. beach
   e. dirty condition, filth
   f. clean condition

D. Using New Words

Write your own sentences using the words from exercise C.

1. _____

2. _____

3. _____

4. _____

5. _____

E. Prepositions of Time

The prepositions at, in, and on are often used to talk about time. **At** is usually used for times on the clock or in the day. **In** is usually used for long periods of time. **On** is used with dates and named days of the week.

> Example: *Please join us **at** noon.*
> *Jean will be back **in** 15 minutes.*
> *I'll see you **on** Tuesday.*

Complete the sentences using at, in, or on.

1. I was born _____ 1975.

2. Yoko goes to school _____ Tuesdays and Thursdays.

3. My bus leaves _____ half an hour.

4. Classes start _____ 7 p.m.

5. She was famous _____ the 1970's.

COMMUNICATING YOUR IDEAS

A. Talk About It

You are the judge! What do you think should happen? Read the scenario. Rank your choices: 1 (first choice), 2 (second choice), 3 (third choice), 4 (last choice). Then work in a group and share your ideas. Give reasons for your choices.

1. Tommy and his friends had a party at the beach. They drank a lot of beer and left their empty cans on the sand. It is against the law to drink on the beach. It is against the law to litter. Tommy and his friends should

   a. _____ Go to jail for a month.

   b. _____ Pay a fine (money).

   c. _____ Pick up trash for a year.

   d. _____ Nothing.

2. Work with your group. Write your own scenario and present it to the class.

ONE STEP BEYOND

■ **Internet**
1. Is there an animal you are afraid of? Is it as dangerous to people as you thought? Research the animal and tell your class about it.
2. Learn more about how to protect our oceans. Find out if there is a beach clean up day in your community. Share the information with your class. Try visiting the Ocean Conservancy website.

■ **Make a News Program**
Make a news program with the top story of Joe's shark attack. Interview the tourist, a paramedic, the doctors and Joe for the top story. Add other stories from the book, along with weather, sports, etc. Videotape the program.

■ **Movies**
Watch a film about ocean life. Some examples are *Whale Rider* and *Free Willy*.

■ **Guest Speaker**
Invite someone from an environmental organization to class to learn more about water pollution. Or invite someone from a rehabilitation center to find out how people learn to live with a disability.

■ **Explore Your Community**
Find out about a volunteer group in your community that works to protect the environment and wildlife. Learn what you can do to help. Share the information with your class.

■ **Journal**
Write about what you learned in this unit in your journal.

■ **Vocabulary**
Copy the words from this unit into your vocabulary logs. Put the words into word groups.

■ **CNN®**
Remember to watch the CNN® video clip for this unit.

A SPORTING LIFE

GETTING READY

1. Write the name of the activity under each picture.

playing tennis   _____   _____   _____

_____   _____   _____

2. Ask a partner about each activity above.

Example: *Do you like playing basketball?*
           Yes I do. / No, I don't.

GRAND SLAM SISTERS

PRE-READING

Discuss in pairs.

1. Do you play tennis? Have you ever played tennis?

2. Do you like watching tennis on TV? Why or why not?

3. Do you know who are the best tennis players in the world right now?

4. What do you know about Venus and Serena Williams?

GRAND SLAM SISTERS

Who has won the most Grand Slam tournaments since 2000? If your answer is a Williams sister, you're right! Between them, sisters Venus and Serena have won all the major tournaments one or more times. They are the first pair of sisters ever to do this. They have won Olympic gold medals, too.

In fact, there are few awards one or the other sister has not won in women's tennis.

Venus was only four years old when her father started to teach her how to hit tennis balls. Her little sister Serena is only fifteen months younger than Venus. Serena wanted to do everything Venus did, so she started hitting tennis balls, too. They both fell in love with tennis. The girls wanted to become professional tennis players. They spent years training and working very hard. They also wanted to have a balanced life. This is very important to the Williams family. Their parents made sure their daughters got a good education. They believe that education and family come first.

continued →

Sometimes Venus and Serena have to compete against each other in singles. Of course, one sister has to win and the other one has to lose. This is very difficult for the sisters, who are also best friends. Venus says, "I want to win, but I want Serena to win, also. I want the best for her." It is easier when they team up together to play doubles. They are an almost unbeatable doubles team, and they enjoy playing together.

The Williams sisters are more than great tennis players. They are smart and artistic young women. They have many other interests. Both young women love fashion, and they design their own tennis clothing. Venus has a degree in interior design and her own interior decorating business. She also loves to cook, surf and play guitar. Serena took acting lessons, and she has already made her Hollywood debut. When she's not playing tennis or acting, she loves to shop for clothing and accessories. She says, "I'm addicted to shopping!" Like most superstar athletes who are also celebrities, Venus and Serena are multi-millionaires. They are role models for kids all over the world, and they participate in many activities to benefit children.

These champion sisters are skilled athletes, but their personalities are very different. Serena shows her emotions while playing tennis. She smiles, she screams and she cries. Venus is quieter. Venus doesn't show her emotions on the tennis court. She keeps her feelings inside. However, their hearts are in the same place. Both sisters are devoted to their family, to their religion, to each other—and of course, to tennis.

Since 2000, the Williams sisters have made women's tennis more exciting and popular. They are strong, beautiful and graceful. They have ruled the tennis world on and off the court. Venus and Serena are double trouble for their opponents, but a double delight for millions of fans and their family.

READING AND WORD STUDY SKILLS

A. Understanding the Main Ideas

Look at the statements below. Circle the correct answer.

1. The Williams sisters have made women's tennis

    a. very boring.   b. very exciting.

2. Venus and Serena are

    a. best friends.   b. actresses.

3. Their personalities are

    a. the same.   b. different.

B. Finding Details

Put a check (✓) under the correct name.

Fact	Venus	Serena
1. She has won Grand Slams.		
2. She won an Olympic gold medal.		
3. She's the little sister.		
4. She loves fashion and designs her own tennis clothes.		
5. She has her own interior decorating business.		
6. She likes to cook, surf and play guitar.		
7. She's addicted to shopping.		
8. She's shows her emotions on the court.		
9. She's quiet on the court.		
10. She's devoted to her family, religion and tennis.		

C. Learning New Words

1. Scan the paragraphs of "Grand Slam Sisters." Write the synonyms from the story to match the underlined words below. The first one is done for you.

Paragraph One

a. ___right___ If your answer is a Williams sister, you're <u>correct</u>!

Paragraph Two

b. _____ They spent years <u>practicing</u> and working very hard.

Paragraph Three

c. _____ Sometimes they have to <u>participate</u> against each other in singles.

Paragraph Four

d. _____ They are <u>intelligent</u>, talented and artistic young women.

Paragraph Five

    e. _____ These champion sisters are both <u>talented</u> athletes, but their personalities are very different.

    f. _____ Venus doesn't show her <u>feelings</u> while playing tennis.

Paragraph Six

    g. _____ They are <u>powerful</u>, beautiful and graceful.

2. Choose five new words from above. Write sentences using both synonyms.

Example: *My brother thinks he is always <u>right</u>.*
He thinks he is always <u>correct</u>.

D. Patterns of Organization

SKILL BUILDER

"Grand Slam Sisters" compares Venus and Serena Williams. To compare means to show the similarities and differences between two or more things. To compare, we use words and expressions such as *both, too, the other one, but* and *on the other hand*. We also use comparatives such as *older than* and *quieter than*.

1. Look back at the reading. Complete the sentences with the correct word or expression.

both (x2)	but	too	the other one	younger than

    a. Her little sister Serena is only fifteen months _____ Venus.

    b. Serena wanted to do everything Venus did, so she started hitting tennis balls _____.

    c. They _____ fell in love with tennis.

    d. Of course, one sister has to win and _____ has to lose.

    e. These champion sisters are _____ amazing athletes, _____ their personalities are very different.

2. Write sentences comparing yourself to a brother, sister or friend. Use some of the words and expressions you learned above.

a. _____

b. _____

c. _____

d. _____

e. _____

E. Drawing Conclusions

Circle the correct answer. Circle T for true, F for false or ITK for Impossible to Know.

1. Venus and Serena have very nice houses.	T	F	ITK
2. They travel internationally.	T	F	ITK
3. Their parents are proud of them.	T	F	ITK
4. They were excellent students in all subjects.	T	F	ITK
5. Venus goes shopping more than Serena.	T	F	ITK

COMMUNICATING YOUR IDEAS

A. Talk About It

Discuss the questions with a small group. Then report back to your class.

1. What are your favorite sports to play? What are your favorite sports to watch?

2. What sports do boys/men often play? What sports do girls/women often play?

3. Do you have a sports hero? If yes, who?

4. What advice do you think the Williams sisters give to young kids about sports and school?

5. Is there a sport that you would like to learn?

6. What other things do you like to do in your free time?

B. Interviewing

Work in a group. Interview each person in your group to complete the chart below. Then present it to the class.

Name	Most popular sports in your country	Your favorite sports	Most famous athlete in your country

TOO MANY COUCH POTATOES

PRE-READING

1. Tennis is a game that many people play to get exercise. Exercise is one important part of a balanced life. Do you get enough exercise?

2. Look at the picture. What is the man doing? Do you think he is healthy?

3. Skim the article quickly. Circle the main idea.

    a. Americans eat too many potatoes.

    b. Americans get enough exercise.

    c. Americans need more physical activity.

READING AND WORD STUDY SKILLS

A. Understanding the Main Ideas

Circle the correct answer.

1. Kiki, the writer, is unhappy because

    a. she is overweight.   b. she is a couch potato.
    c. she has health problems.

2. The government report says that most Americans

    a. get enough physical activity.   b. don't get enough physical activity.
    c. are lazy and fat.

3. Physical activity means

    a. doing sports.   b. walking the dog.   c. both a and b.

4. Kiki wants to

    a. exercise less.   b. exercise more.   c. eat more.

5. The report says Americans should

    a. go to the gym every day.   b. sit and watch TV.
    c. do moderate physical activity every day.

TOO MANY COUCH POTATOES

By Kiki Jones

I just looked in the mirror, and I saw an overweight woman looking back at me. Who is she? Is that really me? I am sad to say I am one of the many Americans who does not do enough physical activity.

Physical activity includes doing things like housework and walking the dog. It also includes doing exercise, such as playing tennis and going to the gym. A government report says that only 1 in 10 Americans do a lot of physical exercise. Three in 10 Americans do very little and 4 in 10 Americans do no activity at all. I am one of the Americans who does very little physical activity.

We have to make more time to work our bodies. Because most Americans don't do enough physical activity, they are in danger of having health problems. We are gaining weight because of too little physical activity. We also eat too many high-calorie foods.

That's a horrible fact.

We really have to get up and get busy! I'm not a couch potato, but my friend Joey is. His idea of exercise is sitting on the sofa, lifting soda cans and potato chips to his mouth while watching other people exercise on TV. I'm not that bad, but I've decided Joey and I are going to change. The report says we should get 30 minutes of moderate physical activity every day to be healthy. Moderate means not too much and not too little. So here are a few simple things we can do:

· Walk up and down the stairs. Don't use the elevator.
· Do gardening.
· Go dancing.
· Play ball with the kids in the park.
· Park the car a few blocks from the office or store, and walk quickly the rest of the way.
· Take a long walk after dinner instead of watching TV.

A little sweat never hurt anyone. In fact, 30 minutes a day can help us live longer and better lives. Let's go!

Pie chart: Very Little 30%, None 40%, Some 20%, Alot 10%

B. Finding Details

1. Find the numbers below in the text. Circle them. Do you know what they mean? Write the number next to the percentage.

1 in 10	3 in 10	4 in 10

a. 10% *1 in 10*   b. 30% _____   c. 40% _____

2. Look at the chart in the article. Write the percentage number (%) next to the statement below.

    a. _____ of Americans do a lot of physical activity.

    b. _____ of Americans do some physical activity.

    c. _____ of Americans do very little physical activity.

    d. _____ of Americans do no physical activity.

3. Look back at the four statements in exercise 2 above. Read the sentences below. Circle the correct answer:

    a. Kiki is an example of statement.   a   b   c   d

    b. Joey is an example of statement.   a   b   c   d

    c. You are an example of statement.   a   b   c   d

C. Learning New Words

Match the word with the definition. Write the letter.

1. _____ overweight   a. a written or spoken statement

2. _____ change   b. heavier than normal

3. _____ enough   c. easy to do

4. _____ couch potato   d. to do something different

5. _____ report   e. as much as needed

6. _____ simple   f. a person who doesn't do any exercise

SKILL
BUILDER

D. Distinguishing Fact and Opinion

1. A fact is something that is true or real. An opinion is what someone believes. Writers give facts in their writing and express their opinions too. It is useful to know the difference between the two.

2. Write F for fact and O for opinion.

    a. _____ 1 in 10 Americans does a lot of physical activity.

    b. _____ I think Americans are fat.

    c. _____ You should not sit on the couch and eat potato chips.

    d. _____ Americans need to exercise more.

e. _____ 30 minutes of exercise a day can help us live longer and better lives.

f. _____ Americans should not eat so many hamburgers, hot dogs and pizza.

COMMUNICATING YOUR IDEAS

A. Talk About It

1. Having a balanced life is important to the Williams family. What is a balanced life? What do *you* need for a balanced life? Circle your choices in the list below.

play sports	work/career	school
exercise	time with family	sleep
religion/spiritual life	study	relaxing
nutrition	time with friends	pets
health	taking care of your home	reading
nature	taking care of children	money
romance	other _____	other _____

2. List the five most important things that you circled above. Write the most important first.

   a. _____

   b. _____

   c. _____

   d. _____

   e. _____

3. In a small group, talk about why these things are important to you for a balanced life. Then share your ideas with the class.

MY ROLE MODEL

PRE-READING

Emile was asked to write an essay about a role model. Emile chose the famous cyclist Lance Armstrong. Scan Emile's report. Complete the chart below as quickly as you can.

Event	Date
1. Lance was born	
2.	1993
3. Lance started the Lance Armstrong Junior Olympic Race Series.	
4. Lance got cancer	
5. Lance set up the Lance Armstrong Foundation	
6.	1999–2004

MY ROLE MODEL

BY EMILE LOPEZ

I have chosen to write about Lance Armstrong. I chose Lance because he is a successful athlete, and he helps other people be successful too.

Lance was born in 1971, in Plano, Texas. He was always competitive and a natural athlete. He loved riding his bicycle. He said that he was "born to race bikes." He also says that his mom, who raised him as a single mother, is his biggest hero. She taught him to never give up.

continued →

In 1993, he started cycling as a professional and became the youngest road racing World Champion ever. Soon he became famous. In 1995 he started the Lance Armstrong Junior Olympic Race Series to support young people's interest in cycling in the United States.

However, one day in 1996, Lance was riding his bike when he collapsed in terrible pain. The doctor told Lance that he had cancer. In the next five months, Lance had two surgeries and chemotherapy. His priorities changed because of his fight with cancer. His experience with cancer gave him the opportunity to appreciate his loving family, close friends and good health.

In 1996, he set up the Lance Armstrong Foundation. It is an organization to help young people and their families manage and survive cancer.

Lance decided to start training seriously again because he was still passionate and dedicated to cycling. Lance is a team player, and his team won the Tour de France every year from 1999 to 2004. The Tour de France is the oldest and most famous cycling race in the world. The race is held in France every summer and takes 21 days to complete. You need to be very fit and healthy to win.

I think Lance is a great role model. He never gives up, he is a great athlete and he helps others. He is an inspiration.

READING AND WORD STUDY SKILLS

A. Understanding the Main Ideas

What happened in Lance Armstrong's life before and after he had cancer?
Put an "X" in the correct column.

Event	Before	After
1. He became famous.		
2. He became the youngest road racing World Champion.		
3. He started the Junior Olympic Race Series.		
4. He was passionate about cycling.		
5. Lance set up the Lance Armstrong Foundation		
6. He won the Tour de France.		

B. Learning New Words

Write the letter of the correct definition next to the word.

1. _____ priorities   a. to be thankful for something

2. _____ appreciate   b. most important things

3. _____ manage   c. a person who works well with others

4. _____ team player   d. to deal with a situation

5. _____ train   e. to prepare by practicing

C. Using New Words

Complete the questions using the words from exercise B. Then ask your partner the questions.

1. Do you always _____ to make time for your priorities?

2. What do people _____ about you?

3. What are the _____ in your life?

4. Are you a _____? Explain.

5. Have you ever _____ for a sport?

D. Understanding Phrasal Verbs

1. Phrasal verbs are very common in English. They are made up of a verb (get, give, take, move, push, etc) and a preposition (on, over, up, with, etc). It is sometimes difficult to know what phrasal verbs mean. You should try to guess the meaning of phrasal verbs in context.

2. Look at the *Newbury House Dictionary of American English* definition below for "give up".

> **22** *phrasal v. insep.* [T] **to give up on s.o.** or **s.t.:** to stop hoping or wishing for s.o. or s.t. to arrive, happen, etc.: *We gave up on the missing mountain climber after he had been missing for 13 days.* **23** *phrasal v. insep.* **to give way:**

3. What did Lance's mom mean when she said, "Don't give up"? Discuss in pairs.

4. There are two more phrasal verbs in the essay. Can you find them?

COMMUNICATING YOUR IDEAS

A. Talk About It

1. Athletes are dedicated to their sports. Learning how to do something well takes a lot of practice and dedication. Talk with your teacher about the personal qualities below. Circle the qualities that are important for athletes.

A good athlete...

is hardworking	is a team player	is talented
is open to new ideas	shows emotions	follows instructions
learns from mistakes	is dedicated	is self-disciplined
is passionate	never gives up	is competitive
is powerful	likes practicing	is smart
has priorities	is artistic	is a role model

2. Which of these qualities are also important for learning a language? Put a check (✓) next to each quality that you think is important for learning a new language. Discuss with your partners why the qualities you checked are important.

B. Write About It

1. What qualities do you have that help you learn English?

   I am a good language learner because I...

   _____

   _____

   _____

2. Look back to Unit 1. What strategies are you using to learn English? Did you reach some of your goals for learning English? Write about it. Share your ideas with your class.

ONE STEP BEYOND

■ **Search the Internet or Library**
Find more information about Venus and Serena Williams, Lance Armstrong or one of your favorite athletes on the Internet or at the library. Find 3-5 new facts about that person, such as his/her favorite hero, other sports that he/she plays, special interests he/she has. Make a short presentation to your class.

■ **Movies**
Movies you might like to watch are *Breaking Away, Field of Dreams, A League of Their Own* or *Hoop Dreams*. Write about what qualities the athletes have.

■ **In the Community**
Find out what physical education classes you can take at your school or in the community. Watch a live game or join a team!

■ **Guest Speaker**
Invite a counselor from your school or community to talk with your class about setting priorities and managing time to have a balanced life.

■ **Journal**
Write about your experiences learning English during this course.

■ **Vocabulary**
Copy the words from this unit into your vocabulary logs. Put the words into word groups.

■ **CNN**®
Remember to watch the CNN® video clip for this unit.

Adjectives

An adjective is a word that describes a noun. Many nouns can be changed into adjectives by adding suffixes to the end of the word. Some suffixes that make adjectives are *−y, −ful* and *−able*.

> It is <u>windy</u> today.   The chair is <u>comfortable</u>.

Adverbs

An adverb is a word that describes a verb. Adverbs answer the question "how?" Many adverbs end with the suffix *−ly*.

> She sings <u>beautifully</u>.   He works <u>quickly</u>.

Nouns and Compound Nouns

A noun is a person, place or thing. *Billy*, *tornado* and *New York City* are nouns. Compound nouns are two nouns that make a new noun. Some compound nouns are *football, teacup* and *bookshelf*.

Past Simple

Use simple past tense for an action completed in the past.

> Juan <u>lived</u> in Chicago for ten years.

> He <u>moved</u> to St. Louis two months ago.

> Yesterday he <u>got</u> a new job at a bank.

There are regular and irregular past verb forms. Regular past verb forms use *−ed* the end to the verb. (Note: Sometimes when adding *−ed* to a verb there is a spelling change.)

> walk–walk<u>ed</u>   live–liv<u>ed</u>   study–studied

For irregular past verbs see the chart on page 131.

For negative sentences and questions in the past tense use *did*.

> Elizabeth <u>did not go</u> to school last week because she was sick.

> <u>Did</u> you <u>get</u> an extra copy of the homework for her?

Past Progressive

Past progressive is formed with *was or were + verb with -ing*.

> *Stephen was dreaming in his morning class.*

> *The other students were studying.*

Use past progressive when two or more actions were happening at the same time in the past.

> *Stephen was dreaming while the teacher was talking.*

Use past progressive when one action was interrupted by another action in the past.

> *Stephen was dreaming when the bell rang.*

Sentence Connectors

There are many kinds of sentence connectors. In this book we practice four connectors:

Because shows reason. It connects two sentences together.

> *I am learning English because I want a better job.*

But shows contrast. It connects two sentences together.

> *My son wants to buy a new car, but he doesn't have enough money.*

So shows result. It can connect two sentences together.

> *I want to learn a lot of English, so I practice every day.*

When shows time. A clause with *when* must be connected to a sentence.

> *When I was a little girl, I liked bubble gum ice cream.*

Verbs

A verb is an action word. We use verbs in many different tenses to show time and time relationships. In English there are regular and irregular verbs in the past tense. Regular verbs use *–ed* at the end of the verb. Irregular verbs use many forms.

In English there are also many phrasal verbs. Phrasal verbs are usually a verb and a preposition together. Together they have a new meaning. Some examples are *get out, come over, speak up* and *pick up*.

IRREGULAR VERB FORMS

be	was	**hear**	heard
become	became	**hide**	hid
begin	began	**hit**	hit
blow	blew	**keep**	kept
break	broke	**know**	knew
bring	brought	**lead**	led
build	built	**leave**	left
buy	bought	**lose**	lost
catch	caught	**make**	made
choose	chose	**meet**	met
come	came	**pay**	paid
cut	cut	**put**	put
do	did	**run**	ran
drink	drank	**say**	said
drive	drove	**see**	saw
eat	ate	**send**	sent
fall	fell	**sleep**	slept
feel	felt	**speak**	spoke
fight	fought	**spend**	spent
find	found	**take**	took
fly	flew	**teach**	taught
forget	forgot	**tell**	told
get	got	**think**	thought
give	gave	**understand**	understood
go	went	**wear**	wore
grow	grew	**win**	won
have	had	**write**	wrote

INDEX OF VOCABULARY

SKILLS INDEX